Merry Christmas 1986

Love from Annie, Jolan & David

OPENING SHOTS
&PARTING LINES

OPENING SHOTS & PARTING LINES

CHARLEY DICKEY

WINCHESTER PRESS
An Imprint of New Century Publishers, Inc.

The publisher and author thank the following publications for graciously allowing the stories in this collection to be used. The stories first appeared in the magazines listed below.

Petersen's Hunting: "Real Men Don't Wear Pantyhose" April, 1974; "A Boy's Best Friend" October, 1974; "Christmas Gift" December, 1975; "The Soil Is Not Deep" May, 1980; "Old Buck and Aunt Sarah" July, 1979; "The Hunter's Call" May, 1978; "My Friend the Tree" November, 1976; "The Truth About My Fear of Cactus" April, 1978; "Before the Saints Come Marching In" September, 1980; "The Linoleum Two-Step" June, 1981; "The Gun-Starers" February, 1975; "Losing Another Crop" March, 1975; "Putting Out the Fire" September, 1974; "Coons Ain't Convenient" April, 1981; "Pen Pals" May, 1981; "Ask a Spider" March, 1976; "Pouring Doubles" October, 1979; "The Long Flight" March, 1978; "The Joy of Whooping" January, 1978; "The Best Part of a Hunting Trip" March, 1979; "My Friend Has Gone" March, 1977; "It Takes Two to Plan a Hunt" December, 1978; "Banking Memories" March, 1974.

Georgia Sportsman: "Bosom Bream" June, 1977; "Just One More Cast" August, 1979; "Canoes Handle Best on Dry Land" July, 1978; "Roughing It Means No Olives" August, 1978; "The Greatest Bass Fisherman" April, 1980; "The Burglar" October, 1980; "On the Trail of Dog-Day Bass" August, 1978; "Training the Outdoor Wife" October, 1978; "How Fish Grow" April, 1977; "How's That Again?" November, 1980; "The Wild Life at Lake Bountiful" June, 1980; "First Aid for Joggers" November, 1978; "Go Easy on the Pyracantha" September, 1979; "Keep a Light Burning" March, 1980; "Secret Baits" July, 1979; "The Rogue" July, 1980; "Generation Gap" September, 1978.

Field & Stream: "Woodcock Can't Read" November, 1981; "On the Antlers of a Dilemma" February, 1983; "That Night Before" March, 1964; "The Best Ways to Hunt Grouse" November, 1978; "Charged by a Dove" September, 1963.

Florida Sportsman: "How to Help a Bird Dog" January, 1982; "Equipped for Quail" February, 1981.

Florida Wildlife: "What Is a Shotgun?" January/February, 1977.

Harris' Complete Deer Hunting Annual 1982: "What Is a Deer Hunter?" (based on Alan Beck's essay "What Is a Boy?")

Copyright © 1983 by Charley Dickey

Printing Code
13   14   15   16

Library of Congress Cataloging in Publication Data

Dickey, Charley.
    Opening shots & parting lines.

    1. Hunting—Ancedotes, facetiae, satire, etc.
2. Fishing—Ancedotes, facetiae, satire, etc.   I. Title.
II. Title: Opening shots and parting lines.
SK33.D535 1983   799'.0207   83-16973
ISBN 0-8329-0313-2

Acknowledgments

There is a bubbling, inexhaustible supply of humor—and quite often some serious philosophical insights—in the people who try to catch fish and hunt birds and animals. From their outdoor adventures they store and treasure many memories, both pleasant and sad. I wish to thank the many generous sportsmen who have shared those memories and given me ideas for stories.

I am particularly grateful to the following people who have helped or inspired me to put words on paper: the late Fred Moses, Charles Elliott, David D. Dickey, Charles Waterman, Bill Rae, John Madson, David Morris, Steve Vaughn, George Martin, Tom Siatos, Ken Elliott, Hugh Gray, Pete Barrett, Duncan Barnes, Jim Rikhoff, Bill Hansen, Gene Smith, Wally Hughes, Morrie Naggiar, Malcolm Johnson, Bill McGrotha, Earle and Bobbie Frye, Vic Dunaway, Bob Elman, Lamar Underwood, Woody Earnheart, Red Chaplin, Bob Bell, Sarah Bartenstein, Bill Sizer, Bill Mitzel, Red Wilkinson, Mary Van Auken, John Logue, Dewey Andrews, Chris Christian, Craig Boddington, Floyd Voight, and others; and from long ago, Dr. Kelleher and Dr. Pierce.

To Bunty,
my best fan

Table of Contents

Preface

Charley Dickey is more interested in people who enjoy hunting, fishing, and camping than in the quarry they pursue or the equipment they use. Something humorous happens on almost every outdoor adventure if the writer can catch it. Quite often, too, the things that happen are worth thinking about. Dedicated sportsmen feel deeply about their outdoor hobbies, and the sentiment a Californian feels for his dog can be understood by another dog owner in New York, if the writer can capture the essence of the emotion.

Dickey, who writes two outdoor columns a week for the *Talla-hassee Democrat,* has been filling the back page for *Petersen's Hunting* under the pen name of Sam Cole since the magazine began publishing a decade ago. He also writes "Parting Line" each month, the back page of Game & Fish Publications' *Georgia Sportsman* and others.

He writes a regular feature for *North American Whitetail* on the misadventures of the "Trophy Buck and Fine Arts Society," much of it about an ancient monster buck that constantly outwits the club members. He continues to write how-to and where-to articles as well as humorous features for *Field & Stream, Outdoor Life,* and many other magazines.

His previous books were on dove shooting, deer hunting, quail hunting, and trout fishing, the last-mentioned with the late Freddie Moses. A limited edition of some of his stories was printed by Jim Rikhoff's Amwell Press in 1977.

Dickey majored in biology and geology at the universities of New Mexico and Tennessee. As a naval pilot during World War II and the Korean conflict, he flew torpedo bombers from several carriers. He has lived in California, Pennsylvania, New England, and various Southern states.

His travels, either for story material or through the courtesy of Uncle Sam, have taken him to Korea, Japan, many Pacific Islands, Mexico, Canada, Central America, and Europe, plus 47 of the 50 states. For a while, he worked for the Tennessee Department of Conservation and then spent a dozen years as a free consultant to hunting preserves as an employee of the Sporting Arms and Ammunition Manufacturers' Institute. For seven years, he was director of the National Shooting Sports Foundation. In 1982, he was presented the Outdoor Writers Association of America's "Excellence of Craft Award," the highest award that organization gives for photojournalism.

A native of Bulls Gap, Tennessee, Dickey travels out of Tallahassee, Florida, to gather pictures and materials for his work as a full-time freelance writer on outdoor subjects. His partner and wife, Bunty, the former Barbara Goddard Theg, is a proper Bostonian who has made a sincere effort to adapt to chiggers, fatback, and people who talk about hunting and fishing all night. They have three grown children—Katie, Steve, and Ellie—who are scattered around the country, and two English setters who sleep where they are most likely to be stumbled over.

OPENING SHOTS
SHOTS
&PARTING
LINES

Real Men Don't Wear Pantyhose

I knew I was getting into trouble when Herman talked me into buying those pantyhose!

There are convenient ways of getting in shape for most hunting trips—climbing steps for grouse hunts or doing arm exercises before paddling a canoe to moose bogs. But there's no way you can get your bottom ready for a pack trip on horseback except by riding a horse.

From my city apartment it's not easy to reach a stable that rents horses, especially at a rate I can afford. One year, before a pack trip for muleys in Wyoming, I rode a bicycle for weeks but it didn't help. Another year I spent a lot of time straddling a motorbike and sliding down bannisters. It didn't get me ready for the saddle torture waiting in Idaho.

You'd think an office job, where you're on and off a chair all day, would prepare your seat for riding a horse. Not one bit. One season I took a sawhorse to the office, put a saddle on it and used it for a desk chair. It might have worked, but secretaries from all over the building kept sneaking in for a look. They'd giggle, rush out the door to get their friends, and you could hear them laughing all the way to the elevator. The boss suggested I remove the contraption, immediately!

If, straight from the city, you've never ridden a pack horse for ten hours, you don't know what pure misery is. It's worse than being sacked all afternoon by the Minnesota Vikings. The next morning you can survive the aches and cramps, but what kills you are the great red patches of chafed skin. It's easier to walk bowlegged all day than to face the mere thought of climbing back on your horse. Even a four-gaited horse doesn't have any easy riding gear if your loins and bottom are chafed raw. Talk about pouring turpentine on an open wound, man, you can't touch your sensitive acreage of chafes with a powderpuff!

The chafing stays with you the whole trip, getting more tender each day. Your muscles break loose every morning about the time the sun comes over the peaks. But if you have a chafing garden, it's just grind, grind, grind all day. It gets to burning so bad you can't think of anything but salves and lotions. If the crew wouldn't get disgusted, you'd be glad to return to camp and hunt jays and magpies, lying flat on your back, of course.

It was my city luncheon friend, Herman, who told me how to prevent chafing. All I had to do was wear a pair of pantyhose. According to Herman the thin layer of nylon slides and prevents friction on vital parts. There's no heating and chafing. Herman is the one who spends his winter weekends in New England hunting for Abominable Snowmen and the summer searching for the Loch Ness monster in Central Park. Herman says he's seen both, many times.

I was planning a trip to Montana's high country and ready to try anything. The more I thought about pantyhose preventing chafing, the better the idea sounded. There was just one catch! Suppose the pack crew saw me putting them on some morning? Or taking them off? I'd be the butt of every trail joke from Yuma to Kalispell. I could hear the wranglers in the bars laughing about the dude who wore pantyhose. By the time the story was told three times, they'd have me wearing a brassiere.

Herman said that was no problem—simply never let the wranglers see me dressing or going to the bathroom in the bushes. Nothing to it.

When I arrived in Whitefish and met the crew, I tried to think of some way to get rid of the three pairs of pantyhose in my duffel. The guide looked like one of the heavies who almost whips Matt Dillon, the wrangler obviously belonged to the Key Hole gang, and the one-eyed Indian cook with the scarred face wore a scalping knife on his belt.

I lay awake all night in the bunkhouse. I desperately wanted to wear those pantyhose but the thought of being caught in them made me cringe. The convincer was the horrible memory of past suffering.

Before anyone stirred, I slipped from my bunk, eased a pair of pantyhose from the cellophane package, and quickly put them on, frantically looking around to see if anyone was watching. After I got them covered with my britches, I was pleasantly surprised how comfortable they felt. Then I woke the others and went outside to check the weather.

We had a good start toward the Continental Divide before the first rest stop. I eased away from the others. My legs and bottom felt great! There was no irritation and outside of a few twinging calf muscles, I felt like I'd been riding on a fluffy pillow. The crew and I warmed up to each other and we joked about the great elk I'd shoot to break the Boone and Crockett record.

You might think it's easy to go to the bathroom away from everyone in the vast wilderness of the big sky country. Just try it! While there's always a certain modesty on the trail, I knew the others were thinking I was unusually shy. Whenever I stood up to leave the campfire, everything seemed to get deathly silent. If I made an excuse to leave the guide, I thought he looked at me rather strangely.

I got a bad run in the first pair of pantyhose and couldn't think of any way to get rid of them. After everyone was asleep, I crawled out of camp and buried the hose like a thief in the night.

The crew must have thought I was the most eager dude they'd ever had. I was always up before anyone else and the last to hit his bedroll. I was careful to keep the spare pantyhose hidden and kept checking my gear. Then I got to worrying that would make them think I was checking to see if they had stolen something.

I worried that I might oversleep and have to get up and dress in front of them and my dreadful secret would be out. Then I got to wondering what would happen if I broke a leg and when they put the splint on they discovered the pantyhose. What if a bear broke into camp and scattered everything and they saw my spare pantyhose? I even crawled out one night to see if anything had dug up that pair I'd buried.

It was the best trail crew I'd ever hunted with but I just knew they were whispering about me. I considered making a clean breast of the whole thing. Around the fire some evening, when everyone was jovial, I'd yank my britches down and holler, "Want to see something funny?"

I thought of confiding in the guide but decided he couldn't keep from laughing. If I tried it with the wrangler, I knew he'd go into hysteria. I considered telling the Indian, saying pantyhose were a spiritual charm in my family. Perhaps he might understand. On the other hand, he might hurt himself rolling on the ground.

I worked myself into a real tizzy and was glad to shoot an elk on the ninth day so we could get out of there. It wasn't a record rack but we were all happy with it. That night, I crawled out and buried the remaining pantyhose, figuring I could get back down the mountain without chafing. I relaxed considerably and was singing as we got to the ranch. I told everybody we'd go to town and the drinks were on me.

They were all for it as soon as they put their horses up and sorted out their gear. I followed them over to the laundry room and watched them put their duds in the electric washer. The guide put in three pairs of pantyhose, the wrangler put in three, and the Indian added four.

Bosom Bream

Like any honest fisherman, I want to know the exact true weight of any outstanding fish I catch.

That doesn't mean that I don't take advantage of certain conditions over which I have no control. For instance, on one lake where I fish there are ten dock operators and each has a set of scales. One manager, Heavy-Hand Harvey, has a set different from the others, graduated to indicate on the heavy side. I have no control over Heavy-Hand.

I don't mind motoring or driving the extra distance to weigh my bass with him. Why should I be different from all the other fishermen on the lake?

Heavy-Hand Harvey has the most popular marina on the lake. I once dropped a shiner on the scales and it pulled three pounds. No wonder I wasn't catching any bass. My bait was too large.

I have never asked Heavy-Hand for any detailed information about how his scales are set. I may suspect that they weigh on the high side but I don't want to know for sure. I do know that if you buy a pound of baloney from him you get two slices. Both of them are transparent.

[7]

It has been my observation that his regular weighers don't ask pointed questions. When you see them motoring several miles to weigh one fish, you know Heavy-Hand has got something going. They sure don't go there for his baloney. It takes three of his pounds to make a decent sandwich. It's cheaper to clean and cook a three-pound shiner.

Of course, I carry one of those pocket spring weighers in my tackle box. It is neatly stored in the same place each time so that it's easy to find after I remove everything else.

The pocket scales instantly indicate if a bass has weight or is lighter than air. I seem to get more favorable weights when I beat the gauge against the gunnels. This really activates it and may have something to do with the five-pound bream I caught last year.

An angler of technical background told me scales weighed heavier in hot weather as the metal expanded. That may be true but it's a lot of trouble to build a fire in your boat.

Sometimes I do not have time to go by Heavy-Hand's, so I drive straight home. We have two sets of scales which I use for weighing exceptional fish.

Our postal scales vary as much as three ounces, or fifty-six cents first class, with a slight atmospheric change. Another handicap is that the scales only weigh up to sixteen ounces, hardly enough to weigh the eyeballs of the striped bass I catch. This forces me to do some interpolation. I ask myself how much it would cost to mail the fish first class and then divide by twenty. This gives me the number of ounces and all I have to do then is divide by sixteen.

The other scales are a set of the bathroom kind which you stand on but if you have a large stomach you cannot see the dial. It has a mysterious defect known as creep. For instance, I weigh each night before going to bed. The next morning I ease up on the scales to see if I lost ten pounds during the night. I never have but there's no harm in looking.

The creep in the scales is confusing. Frequently it shows that I *gained* five pounds overnight. How could anyone swallow that much oxygen?

This phenomenon of weight increase overnight has created marital problems. My wife insists that I have been slipping into the kitchen and compiling triple-decker peanut-butter sandwiches. She has taken to putting marks on jars and cans, the same as some people mark booze bottles to see how much the maid is sneaking.

In the fertile private ponds along the Georgia-Florida border there is a species called the bosom bream. This is the quaint native name given to bream so large the only way you can hold them is to clasp them to your bosom. Some locals use a variation.

Anyway, recently I came home with five of the largest bosom bream I've ever caught. Before putting them into a drum of formaldehyde to ship them to the Smithsonian Institution, I decided to weigh them.

No one was at home to help me hold the fish on the bathroom scales. I decided the only way to weigh was to hold them and then stand on the bathroom scales, after first weighing myself. As it was necessary to clutch them to my bosom. I took off all my clothes to keep them from getting messed up.

Unfortunately, the light was out in the bathroom so I moved the scales to the foyer near the front door. It is quite possible you have never tried to weigh five monster bream this way. It's not easy. Just as you get them carefully cuddled, one or two will slip and splatter the floor.

Finally, I got a firm grip on four with the fifth clenched in my teeth, and stepped on the scales ready to read the total weight. That's when the doorbell rang, only a few feet from my head.

In my unbalanced condition, I don't recall what I mumbled but the door opened and there stood two young ladies with brief cases.

Looking back on the situation, I don't know what I should have said. One does feel compelled to say something. I doubt if any of the etiquette books explain the introductory procedure of two strange women to a naked man clasping five bream. How does one really know who should speak first?

Unclenching my teeth and letting one bream drop, I said, "I'm a member of Weight Watchers."

Perhaps this was not a satisfactory explanation as they simply stood there. Apparently they expected to be invited inside. Finally, one of them took a step forward and said, "We'd like to interview you. We're doing a sociological survey for a doctoral thesis at the University of Georgia."

The other one added, "You are the most promising candidate we've met. May we come in?"

I mumbled, "Do you want me with the fish or without?"

As I stepped off the scales, I asked, "By the way, what's your thesis about?"

The first one smiled, "Sex habits of the married suburban male."

A Boy's Best Friend

When you were a small boy did you ever sneak your dog into your bedroom? Or up on the bed with you?

What? You mean you never owned a dog when you were growing up? Why, sir, there is nothing in this vast world like your first dog!

You have missed one of the greatest joys on earth. To whom did you turn in time of trouble? When as a small lad in some mischief you were sent to bed without supper, who was there to comfort you? When your father's stern face frowned at you for some minor sin of youth, and your mother put on a show of displeasure so as not to further arouse him, did you not have a dog to slip in the back stairs to help you through the long night?

When your world came crashing down on your shoulders, when even your brother and sister looked away with smug disgust, did you not have a small puppy to cling to?

When all you knew had cast against you, there was warm solace in pulling your hunting companion under the covers. True, it was necessary to quiet his joyous yelps at the chance to be with you. But with what mysterious senses he perceived your distress, your special time of trouble. He nestled close to you, silently licking your cheek to let you know he understood. When all others had forsaken you, he would still be your friend. He asked only for a chance to share the long night while you lay sleepless wondering what bad marks were being put on your slate in heaven and if your pranks had condemned you to eternal hellfire.

While the authorities who controlled your daily life were displeased with you, the small setter eagerly sought your companionship. He accepted you just as you were, with all of your sins and faults. Of all in life you knew, he alone did not judge you. It mattered not to him what you had done, or might do in the future. And though you did not realize it then, his soft body was filled with a deep wisdom. Everything in the past was gone and he had no worries for the future. He lived each second as it came, asking no more. He felt your sadness of the moment and was happy to let you draw strength from his presence. Second by second you lay quietly together.

Your vivid imagination, not yet tarnished by cynicism and the fear of being laughed at, soared into the future. You and Pepper would run away together. You would not even leave a note, but simply disappear. Your family would grieve for you. They would be sorry they had sent you to bed without supper.

Years would drift away and the family would have given you up as lost forever. Then, one day you'd come riding back to town in a long car with a chauffeur, the mysterious but powerful oil magnate who controlled the destinies of men and nations. Beside you on the plush seat would be Pepper, wearing a collar of diamonds—the one friend who had remained loyal. But you'd be charitable with the family, carry no grudges. You would not only forgive them but shower them with presents. They would shed tears of joy to see you and beg you to stay with them forever.

As the vision reached its peak, and you were gently sinking into sleep, there was a quiet tap-tap on the door. It slowly opened, the old hinges squeaking in protest. A shadowy form drifted through the dark. Where the moon rays sifted through the curtains, a hand with a plate appeared, followed by your mother in her flowery dressing gown. She gently called your name and asked if you were sleeping.

You and Pepper sat up together, his body wiggling, for he had smelled the sandwich, cookies, and milk. Your mother put her soft hand on your tousled hair, whispered that she loved you and tomorrow would be a new day and backed toward the door and closed it. In the hall, she looked up at your father and they both smiled, but you did not know that for many years.

Although your pride had been shattered, you were not so wounded that the smell of ham and oatmeal cookies didn't remind you of the rumblings of your empty stomach. You scrooched over to the nightstand, grabbed the sandwich and took a huge bite, savoring the homemade bread. You washed it down with a gulp of milk and took another bite.

But something was wrong. A pair of moist, brown eyes were staring at you, silently pleading for a morsel. How quickly we forget, when all goes well. In time of sorrow, we cry for succor from any source; in prosperity, we do not need to share. How strange that the only companion in the world a few moments before should so quickly be forgotten.

Your eyes glance toward the ceiling and you know one of St. Peter's angels has scored another mark against you. Perhaps the recording angel is weary and has not yet noticed. You hastily break the sandwich in two, using your fingernails to pinch through the ham. You proffer it quickly to the setter who's now standing up in your bed, tail merrily wagging. He takes your offering and hunkers down to enjoy it. A singular being, you think. He would have thought none the less of you if you had given him nothing.

Your spirit revived from the sandwich, you sit on the edge of the bed and share the cookies, two for you and two for Pepper. As the hunger leaves, you let your head fall back on the downy pillow. You know that you should get up and brush your teeth but your mind is flickering with greater things. How, you wonder, does a dog get to heaven?

Yes, sir, if you have never had a hunting dog, then you have missed out on a great part of life. It is as though you had been born without sight or hearing, or only half a heart. Once you have had a dog, you will have many more. Though some may hunt better than others, or do this and that, there will never be but one first dog. He will be with you always, in a special place, where no other dog or person can intrude. A little secret place which no one knows about and sometimes you are afraid to go there yourself because you cannot control the tears.

Just One More Cast

"**J**ust one more cast" has caused more arguments and divorces than anything pertaining to fishing.

It's the kind of statement that keeps a boat on the water past midnight when both anglers were due home shortly after sunset.

Fishermen are subject to strange hunches. Unknown tongues in the brain keep babbling that the fish are about to turn on. One more cast and Old Pile-Driver will strike.

The flashes of intuition really don't make sense. The anglers have been fishing five hours at a rate of three casts a minute. They have gone through every lure in their tackle boxes. They have given the fish every opportunity, but none has accepted their offerings. Why does the angler think one more cast will cause the fish to change their minds?

There's nothing dependable about fish. You can't put any stock in what they're supposed to do. There's no reason to have any faith or trust in them. If they turn on at all, it's when you're at the office. Every angler knows that there is only one reliable thing about fish:

They hit the day before you arrive and the day after you leave.

A few years ago, I went fishing with a friend on Friday for an afternoon trip. He kept saying, "Just one more cast," and the first thing I knew it was Monday morning. The only break he took was to rush home on Sunday because he was a deacon in the church. After the service, he came running back to the boat. I asked him what the preacher talked about. He said, "Cast thy bread upon the waters and have faith."

I guess my buddy got mixed up. I tried baiting with bread balls and couldn't get even a minnow to hit. He said there was no reference made to spinners, crankbaits, or spoons.

As near as I can tell, there's no such thing as "Just one more cast." If your buddy doesn't catch a fish, he's unhappy and wants to try it again. If his hooks get tangled in a fish, he says, "We can't leave now! They're just starting to feed."

I have one buddy who insists on casting around pilings while I'm docking the boat after a long day of exercising my casting arm. He did that one night ten years ago and landed a five-pound bass. It was the worst thing that ever happened to him, or me. No one has caught a bass at that dock since the freak accident, but my buddy tries it every time.

I got mad at him one evening and drove home and left him. I woke up at daybreak and my conscience was bothering me. I drove back to the dock and was considerably relieved to find him. He was still casting. Without turning his head, he asked, "Where you been?"

He hadn't caught a fish. I asked him to get in the car because I had to go to work. He replied, "Just one more cast."

Based on three casts per minute for twelve hours of fishing, I calculated that he had made 2,160 casts, or 2,150 if he stopped to go to the bathroom a couple of times. He had not gotten a strike. Why did he figure one more cast would catch a fish?

Well, nobody ever said there was anything logical about a fisherman, especially another fisherman. If each cast averaged forty-five feet, he covered 96,750 linear feet, or more than eighteen miles, with his lures. No fish interrupted the retrieves. Yet he thought that with one more cast he would get a strike.

When I finally insisted that I had to go to work, he said, "Go ahead. Forsake your old buddy. I'll bum a ride back to town."

There comes a time when you have to quit fishing. If you don't, how can you go on another trip? When you visit the homes of fishermen, it is customary for them to take you into their dens where mounted fish cluster the walls. Your host will invariably point to the most prized mount and say, "I caught him on the last cast."

I do not know why they insist on lying. I know the proper etiquette when someone shows me a trophy fish. I know how to open my mouth and gasp in awe and wonderment. With great admiration, I ask how long it took to land the monster, where he was fishing and with what lure. I do this with everyone. In case I ever catch a trophy, they'd better do the same for me. That is, if they ever expect me to speak to them again.

It is not necessary for them to embellish their stories by saying the prize was caught on the last cast. Besides, it's an outright lie! When you hit the jackpot on a slot machine, you traditionally put another coin in to pull off the three bars. If you don't, you'll never hit a jackpot the rest of your life.

It is physically, mentally, morally, and spiritually impossible for an angler to catch a trophy on his last cast of the day. He is compelled to cast again to see if there is an even bigger one out there. He has to do it! He has no control over the situation.

Recently, a friend of mine phoned when I was not at home and left word for me to call him immediately upon my return. It was an emergency. I rushed to the phone with dire thoughts of an accident, such as a boat being launched with the plug out.

My buddy had just returned from Central Florida where he had caught a largemouth bass weighing 13 pounds, 2 ounces on a black Jitterbug. My best guess is that it did not take him more than two hours to tell his story. Then he added, "I caught him on the last cast."

After suitable exclamations about his skill, I asked, "You mean you didn't cast again to see if there was another bass?"

"That's right," he replied. "I'd swear on a stack of Bibles I caught him on my last cast."

"That's horrible," I screamed. "Don't you know that largemouth bass weighing 13-2 travel in schools with bass weighing 15 pounds?"

He shouted back, "Well, if they do they sure didn't hit my black Jitterbug."

Woodcock Can't Read

The woodcock has a lot of trouble making up his mind which escape route to take when flushed by hunters. He selects a resting site with an infinite number of exit possibilities. Until the woodcock is disturbed, he really doesn't know where he will fly. If the bird doesn't know, how can the hunter possibly know?

New England writers have written most of the articles about woodcock hunting. They are honest enough, but the trouble is that the woodcock haven't read the articles. For instance, no North-eastern article would be complete without a description of how a flushing woodcock towers above the alders, hovers an instant, and then pours on the coal. On my first woodcock adventure in Maine many years ago, I was delighted when the first bird flushed vertically until he cleared the ten-foot alders. For a brief instant, the woodcock hovered. I led him the same way I would a target nailed to a post. The bird crumpled and I yelled "Fetch" to the English setters with an unnecessary tone of "I shot, didn't I?"

Since I am an expert shot with my 20-gauge shotgun at stationary targets no more than twenty yards distant, my mind danced with visions of filling the limit of five woodcock with five shells. A few minutes later, the dogs locked up and I walked in with my partner. There was a large opening in the alder canopy above where the woodcock had to be squatting. Since it was obvious the flushed bird would make for the opening, I locked my mind on it and got ready to shoot another hovering woodcock.

There was some rustling in the dry leaves and my partner shot. I held my gun ready, waiting for the woodcock to appear in the opening. When nothing appeared for several seconds, my partner said, "Are you posing for a picture? The woodcock is gone."

He explained that the woodcock had been a grasscutter, barely clearing the weeds and grass as he wove in and out of the alders. The next four birds we flushed stayed below the canopy, and my shooting average took a nose dive.

While a woodcock ascending almost vertically gives you time to set your watch before firing, those that take off low and zigzag through the cover seem to disappear with the speed of light. There is time for only one fast shot before the bird is gone.

The fastest woodcock of all is one that heads toward you after your buddy bumps it. There may be time for a number eight low-house shot. On the other hand, you may get only a glimpse of a brown fuzz of feathers. Twice my companion hollered to ask why I didn't shoot. My weak reply was that I thought the birds were brown thrashers.

You can't put much stock in the consistency of woodcock. When I first began hunting them, I thought perhaps the birds fed on fermented berries and got drunk like robins and waxwings sometimes do. Then I read that woodcock only eat earthworms, and for a while I thought that the worms were eating fermented berries. Further study revealed that a woodcock may eat half or even all of its body weight in worms each day. That would explain the erratic speed and flight pattern of a departing woodcock. An empty woodcock, with no extra ballast, would depart on full throttle. One bogged down with worms would be a slow starter with a tendency to hover. It was a good theory, but I have been unable to put it to practical advantage. I could never train my dogs to point only woodcock loaded down with earthworms.

Over the years, of course, I have learned how one should deal with woodcock. One of Charley's Laws states that a hunter approaching a dog pointing a woodcock should never make up his mind how the bird will flush. Further defined, the Law states that if a hunter gets his mind locked on one pattern of departure, the bird will invariably do something different. This goes back to the fundamental principle that a woodcock doesn't really know where he's going until he gets airborne. If the bird doesn't know, how can the hunter know?

The proper approach to a pointing dog is to come in from behind with a vacant mind. Do not let woodcock lore clutter your thoughts. Do not anticipate how the woodcock will flush. No matter how tempting the overhead openings, the bird may never reach an altitude of four feet when he abruptly changes direction. The only way to handle a shot is to take it as it develops.

There is a great deal of lore and tradition connected with woodcock hunting in northern regions. For instance, hunters in New England, Pennsylvania, Michigan, and Wisconsin spend considerable time arguing about whether they're shooting at flight birds or native-bred woodcock. There is so much speculation about migratory woodcock that I sometimes wonder if the hunters have been eating fermented berries. I have no strong feelings about the matter. When a woodcock flushes, I don't stop to consider if it's a local or imported bird. I'm not prejudiced.

After more than twenty years of association with a variety of woodcock hunters, I have yet to meet one who could look at a dead woodcock and tell if it was a domestic bird or one just passing through. What it boils down to is this: If hunters find a lot of birds, the flights are in; if they don't find many birds, the flights haven't come down yet. Sometimes they still say this in December with a foot of snow on the ground.

For years, Southerners assumed the woodcock they hunted were all migratory; there wasn't a lot of chatter about local and imported birds. Now, wildlife biologists at Auburn University and the University of Georgia have discovered considerable nesting in Alabama and Georgia. That proves two things: Nobody knows as much as they think they do about woodcock, and not everyone at those schools goes out for football.

It's just a question of time before hunters from Louisiana to South Carolina will be staying up nights wondering if they're shooting indigenous woodcock or foreigners. Some will probably worry about their daughters if mixed woodcock are served for dinner.

There was one period in my woodcock career when I was shooting fairly well, sometimes running as many as two straight. Then a

Minnesota specialist infected me with a dose of woodcock lore. He read British magazines and had hunted European woodcock in Ireland and Brittany. That made him a qualified expert, and I listened to him eagerly.

The gist of his observations and studies was that nine out of ten flushing woodcock would extrude a lime sprinkle about the time they reached optimum distance for an improved cylinder choke. It was not clear if the woodcock splattered from fright, derision, or as a diversionary tactic. He was utterly appalled when I admitted that I had never observed this flight characteristic. As he rubbed the medallions on his tweed hat, I could see that he was convinced I would never make it as a woodcock hunter. Anyway, he asked my help in keeping a record of deposits made by flushing woodcock.

In most woodcock coverts, one is fairly busy when a bird flushes. Depending on the type of cover and its arrangement, the hunter has from one to three seconds to fire before the bird disappears or is out of range. In addition to concentrating on his shooting, the hunter must keep an eye on his dog's performance. Also, he must watch his companion's dog for mistakes in case this information is needed later. Watching and waiting for lime sprays from a frantic woodcock is bound to crowd activities. In fact, I quickly discovered that it completely threw my shotgun timing off.

Quite often, just when I wanted to pull the trigger, there was not the faintest trace of a white spot in the woodcock's slipstream. As I relaxed, the woodcock would suddenly zig around a tree, but not before, at the last possible instant, dropping a lime bomb. It was then too late to shoot. Although the observations wrecked my shooting, I faithfully kept records for a few hunts. Then I began keeping records of a different sort and finally wrote my tweedy friend. It was a one-line report: "I have been shooting the lime out of woodcock but have not recorded any deposits from falling woodcock or after they hit the ground."

In New England woodcock hunters have created a subculture of addicts who hoard secret coverts. Regardless of what the birds are doing, they return to the same coverts each year. Fred Baird, a collector of such treasures in Maine, was kind enough to take me to some of his troves. Once I got used to being blindfolded, I didn't mind the long drives between locations. On arriving at a patch of alders, Fred would dash into the thicket to see if cows had grazed out the ground cover and if there were fresh lime splashes and woodcock drillings. If the signs were right, Fred would put the belled dogs down.

Since the coverts were seldom more than two or three acres, it didn't take long for the dogs to tinkle out the territory. I finally figured why Fred was willing to drive miles to a secret habitat. If birds happened to be there, he received high praise and considerable glory for his knowledge of woodcock. If there were no birds, Fred filled the void with stories of woodcock he had found there in previous years. There was no question about his devotion to history. He could tell you how many woodcock Benedict Arnold put up in that very covert on his way to Quebec. With all the history recitation and the speculation on flight birds, the first thing I knew, we had driven another sixty miles to a secret covert.

Fred was as fine a host as I have ever hunted with. But during my third season with him, it occurred to me that we were driving about 300 miles a day from one remote pocket to another. We started before dawn and returned after dark, yet the total hunting time was no more than forty-five minutes. After Fred got so he would trust me without the blindfold, I noticed that we passed hundreds of alder thickets. In fact, you can spit anywhere in the southern half of Maine and hit an alder thicket. They all looked alike to me. I asked Fred why some of the clumps didn't have woodcock.

He gave me a withering look, as if I had asked him to go to the bank and take out some of his principal, or suggested that the Atlantic salmon was a rough fish. He patiently explained that tradition demanded that a woodcocker hunt the same coverts year after year. It was the stylish thing to do and if you didn't, you wouldn't have anything to talk about all winter. I tried to tell Fred that a woodcock doesn't care anything about tradition, lore, or history. It's a pretty simple bird and all it wants is a convenient supply of worms, a protected place to sleep, and freedom to make lime deposits. One alder thicket might be as good as the next one.

Fred said there was no help for me, so I left and drove over to a lodge on Damariscotta Lake. The main agricultural crop was alders and the next morning I put my old setter down and followed him. By 10 A.M. I was back at the lodge with my limit. There were woodcock all over the place. I phoned Fred and invited him to join me. He asked if they were local or flight birds. I asked what difference that made. Fred said he had never thought highly of the cover "down to Damariscotta." I replied that the cover wasn't trying to win a popularity contest and that it was full of woodcock. Fred said I had lucked into flight birds and he didn't care to hunt coverts he didn't know the history of.

I don't particularly care how I locate woodcock. For the next three days, I found so many birds I forgot to stop and look for lime splashes and bill borings, and I never got more than two miles from the lodge. I learned from the lodge owner that no one from Maine ever hunted there. I guess nobody ever got started and there was no tradition.

Part of woodcock lore is that the birds always hold tight for a pointing dog. Quail hunters don't like their dogs working woodcock because they can be crowded and the dogs are liable to get to thinking they can do the same with bobwhite coveys. Well, most of the time woodcock do sit well for a dog. That is, when they're not running ahead. Some woodcock don't care at all for a dog's hot breath.

One of the best woodcock dogs I ever hunted with was a Brittany in Louisiana named Pierre. We hunted sedge and scrub, upland openings, and swamps with him. When a woodcock flushed and shots rang out, Pierre came back with the game. Sometimes he stayed gone for an awful long time, but when he came back he had something—a turtle, an armadillo, or a woodcock. Pierre's Cajun owner was a practical hunter. He explained that it was customary in his parish to teach the dogs that it was in their best interest to retrieve.

It was a tradition I could understand and appreciate. I asked the Cajun how he trained Pierre. He replied, "I use what you call zee reward seesteem when training zee dog to retrieve. If he fetch eet, he ees rewarded by not getting zee wheeping!"

Christmas Gift

Nobody could figure out what to give old Odes Puckett for Christmas and him lying up in that walnut four-poster gasping for breath and not likely to see another spring.

I reckon you've heard of Odes. If you ain't, you ain't a bear hunter. He's bred and trained more bear dogs than anybody north of hell. Old Odes run hounds for the Skint Knee Club more than sixty years and has peeled more bear hides than anybody in the Snowbird Mountains.

Odes broke in most of the hounds in this country and most of the hunters, too. He had to give it up on his eightieth birthday and it tore him up.

Ever since he took to bed Odes got worse, lying there losing flesh and his bald head shrinking until he looked like a sick turkey gobbler. Nothing would perk him up, even his wife Katy Sue, who nursed him and give him tonic, buttermilk, and cornbread.

I guess it was Grover Casson who come up with the idea of breathing some fire into Odes and making it a big Christmas. You can always count on Grover. I've seen him fight his way through six berserk dogs to get at a bear and cut its throat. Anyway, Grover sent word for us to meet at Shot Beech cabin and he give us his plan.

About a dozen of us met below Odes's cabin near midnight Christmas Eve. Course we had let Katy Sue in on what we was doin'. Grover had a yearling bear on a chain and he had a license for it.

Grover sent me up to sneak into Odes's backyard and leash up the only two hounds Odes had left. Old Blue Jack and Troop were about as dried up as Odes and they didn't raise no fuss when I come into their pen and took them over to my house.

Grover's plan was to lead that bear in a circle a half mile from Odes's cabin, then swing in and make another circle a quarter mile away and the third circle right around the yard. It had rained for three days before Christmas Eve and it was easy to lay a trail. That's what they done but I guess the boys was nipping and after they made the last circle Grover got the idea of taking that bear up on the front porch and through the house, Katy Sue being half deaf and Odes half dead.

Christmas morning come off cold with just a bit of breeze sifting down into the cove. There must have been fifty bear hunters met at the foot of the cove late in the morning about eight o'clock, even some from across the Smokies that old Odes had took lost dogs to when they come through the gap. I never seen so many bear dogs. They was Plotts, Walkers, redbones, blueticks, and crosses with Airdale, pit bull, and terrier.

Half of the hunters went up to wish Merry Christmas to Odes and the rest of us stayed with the dogs. They come back and then we went up. Odes was lying there propped up. It didn't take but one look to tell that he didn't care whether Christmas kept or not. It was all he could do to get up enough steam to say howdy.

About that time the dogs was led up to the outer circle of the bear trail and cut loose and you could hear the strike dogs. Grover, standing near Odes, cupped his ear and said, "Hush everybody. I believe I hear dogs running. Who do you suppose would be running dogs on Christmas Day?"

I opened the window and let the cold air and dog chorus in. I never heard such music in my life. It sounded like the whole cove was full of dogs. I looked over at Odes and a glimmer of light had come in his faded eyes.

It was deathly quiet in that room. Nobody dared breathe too loud and disturb the hound music. You could follow that pack every step of the way.

The dogs swung in on the quarter-mile circle and I saw old Odes jerk up straight and pull the covers down and kinda lean into the sounds. He kept leaning toward that open window until I thought he was going to fall out of bed and I took hold of him and propped him up again.

When that pack was almost around the circle, my boy Cleve cut loose old Blue Jack and Troop on the inside circle around the yard to give them a start. When they struck and yelled, old Odes come up out of that bed right on his feet. He started jumping up and down on that cane mattress in his long handles and there was no way to stop him.

Old Odes come down off of that bed and stuck his head out the window and you could have heard him on the other side of the Big Smokies. "Who-ee-ee, speak to him boys! Who-ee-ee, Blue Jack! Who-ee-ee, Troop!"

Old Odes turned to us and shouted, "Godamighty, boys, where's my britches? Blue Jack and Troop are leading the biggest passel of hounds ever been in these hills!"

The pack caught up with Blue Jack and Troop and the whole bunch was falling all over each other coming through the yard headed for the porch. Nobody thought to open the front door but there wasn't time anyway. Old Odes was whooping them on as bodies thumped against the front door and you could hear claws scratching and a few dogs biting one another in the excitement.

When the front door give, about twenty dogs in a squirming ball were fighting to get through and when the dam broke they was dogs all over the house. I heard Katy Sue scream, "I knew those hounds would be the death of me!" I rushed into the kitchen and Katy Sue was dancing on top a high stool. A bluetick hit it and when the stool and Katy Sue caved in I caught her and stood her on the sink.

Grover was grabbing dogs and tossing them left and right. Finally he reached the back door and opened it and ran out in the yard and hollered, "Who-ee-ee!" The dogs tumbled and piled out after him and Grover got knocked down three times before the dogs took up the mountain.

Old Odes was still jumping up and down on the bed. He yelled, "Who-ee-ee! Speak to him Blue Jack! Merry Christmas! Godamighty, where's my gun, boys? Merry Christmas! Who-ee-ee-ee-ee!"

By New Year's we rounded up every one of them dogs and the last I heard from old Odes was he sent word to everybody he was looking for a couple of pups. Who-ee-ee!

*What Is a Deer Hunter?**

Between a boy's first rifle and the tottering of an old man we find a peculiar creature called a deer hunter. They come in assorted sizes, but they all have the same creed: to rush to the woods when the deer season is open and enjoy every second of each hunting trip—and when it's past time to go home to tell just one more story.

Deer hunters are found nearly everywhere—trying to walk through the woods on dry leaves without crackling, freezing in tree stands, bogged down in swamps, puffing up steep mountains, turning off alarm clocks at four in the morning, and telling hunting stories at business meetings. Mothers love them, young girls can't understand them, wives give up on them, the boss envies them, and Heaven helps them. A deer hunter is Truth with blistered feet, Beauty caught in a driving rain, Optimism with the odds against him, Wisdom with a love of nature, and the Hope of the future with good will toward mankind.

*Based on Alan Beck's essay, "What Is a Boy?"

When you are busy, a deer hunter is thinking of old logging trails, backpacking gear, and country roads. When you want him to make a good impression on someone, all he can talk about is rubs, scrapes, the rutting season, and reloads.

A deer hunter is a paradox in old clothes—he eats Vienna sausage and rat cheese at a country store, but at home he's on a special diet; he can sit in a tree stand for hours without going, but at home he has weak kidneys; he has the energy of a hurricane when scouting for bucks but hires the neighbor's kid to mow the lawn; and he has the imagination of a scientist as he hunts for an old buck that'll make the Boone and Crockett records.

A buck hunter has the courage of a lion as he sits quietly shivering in pre-dawn sleet; he has the enthusiasm of a firecracker as he follows big tracks in the snow made by a doe; and when a big Christmas-tree buck jumps out of his bed, the hunter has forgotten to load his rifle.

He likes sloppy britches with plenty of seat room, waterproof boots, longhandles, camouflage caps, frequent holidays, vacations during the deer season, and questionable companions who are also deer hunters. He's not much for social gatherings, posted land, kin folks who visit on weekends, neckties, litterers, double pay on Saturdays and Sundays, or neighbors who don't hunt. Without thought of race, creed, or color, he likes people who hunt deer during the season and talk about it the rest of the year.

Nobody else is so early to rise, or so late straggling back to town. Nobody else gets so much fun from icicle ears, frozen toes, and aching legs. Nobody else suffers so patiently with a sore hind end, chapped lips, and blistered heels. Nobody else can cram so much into one hunting coat—the wrong topo map, a compass that doesn't work, a small flashlight with dead batteries, wet matches in a waterproof container, a salami-and-onion sandwich from three seasons ago, a leaky vial of doe scent, two boxes of loose rattling cartridges, and a copy of the hunting regulations from five years past.

A deer hunter is a magical creature—you might get sore at his constant chatter about Solunar Tables but you can't lock him out of your heart. When the bucks are rutting, don't expect him to show up at Sunday school, birthday parties, or anniversaries. He'll do more than his share of work on the job but he'll vanish when the season rolls around. There's only one remedy for deer addiction.

You might as well give up—the deer hunter is a child of nature with a hopeless one-track mind. He'll always be slow about yard work when hunting season opens. And you may as well quit trying to understand why he needs another rifle when his closet is jumbled full with them. Just forget about hot dinners and leave his in the oven.

And though you get sore at him at times, you know you'll always like him. There's something about him that rings true, that you can really count on. He's a simple and kindly man who only asks that wildlife have the habitat it needs, that the bucks grow old and big, and that he's out there with them when they're moving.

Canoes Handle Best on Dry Land

There's nothing wrong with a canoe that a lot of dry land won't cure!

Several of my strange friends are always trying to get me to go fishing in a canoe. As far as I know, I've never done anything to harm *them*.

My main objection to canoes is that you never have any warning before you get baptized. You're sitting comfortably enjoying the fishing until all of a sudden your buddy takes a deep breath and before you know what happened you're treading water. There's no proper time to prepare for conversion.

There's nothing wrong with canoes that a seven-foot keel couldn't fix. What do the canoeists have against flatbottoms? Haven't they ever seen a johnboat?

The canoe paddlers start off with two strikes against them. With that round bottom, it's not a question of *if* the canoe will roll over but *when!* What you do most on a river trip is try to dry out.

Maybe that's why I'm not keen on overnight canoe trips. I've never had the pleasure of sleeping in a dry bedroll. What I mostly do is build fires, hang canvas, strain river water out of hamburger, and try to keep powdered food from blowing up.

Recently, when I wasn't bothering a living soul, a buddy came by and talked me into a four-day canoe trip. He caught me at a vulnerable moment. My wife wanted the garage painted.

I agreed to the trip with one stipulation. We would camp the first night at the launching point. I wanted to see what it was like to camp with dry gear.

The next morning we must have gone a hundred yards downstream before the canoe did a snap roll. I grabbed my tackle box and rod with one hand and held the canoe with the other. As on other occasions, I noted that the assorted gear did not float at the same speed.

For instance, my unencumbered life jacket floated high with the current and sped happily ahead of the bedroll wrapped in a plastic garbage bag. In a few minutes, we could see our gear bobbing happily as it strung out for a quarter of a mile. I was not worried about recovering it because fishermen are good about retrieving salvage and returning it to drenched owners. However, I did become upset when a wildlife officer motioned me ashore and gave me a citation for littering.

When we finally recovered all of the gear about five miles downstream, after jolly remarks by fishermen, we pulled onto a sandbar to build a fire and spread gear. As is customary during these circumstances, that's when the thunderstorm hit.

There is one thing about staying soaked for three solid days. It makes you appreciate good roofing material.

Perhaps you've never had the pleasure of fishing from a loaded canoe. It's roughly equivalent to trying to fish while hang gliding.

One buddy of mine says he likes canoe fishing because it's a return to primitive conditions. Well, Indians were tougher than we are. Besides, they ran around nearly naked and didn't have much gear. It wasn't any inconvenience at all for them to roll a canoe. I'll tell you one thing, the only Indian I've seen lately on the water was sitting in the middle of a Boston Whaler listening to his CB.

I once had the misfortune to ride in a genuine Indian canoe in Quebec. It was made of birch bark circling a flimsy frame of hacked limbs. There was no seat. You placed your knees on one frame, your feet on the one behind, and hunkered down trying not to kick a hole in the birch.

The only reason I consented to venture onto water in this awkward position was because we had hiked three miles to catch a monstrous trout that reportedly had been feeding on baby moose and the canoe was the only available conveyance. Hunched down in the canoe, my knees lasted exactly twenty minutes. When my buddy refused to return to shore, I leaned slightly, rolled the canoe over, and swam for it. No brown trout was worth the agony of that canoe.

I'm not saying that taking a canoe trip isn't a lot of fun. It can be hilarious. Several years ago, my friend Fred and I chartered a canoe and equipment from Cliff Wold in Ely, Minnesota, for a five-day smallmouth trip. Cliff gave us a map, and we started out.

About three hours later, I found out what the word "portage" on a map means. It means you have to pick up all your gear *and* the canoe and tote them across dry land until you hit water. It was quite a shock to discover that this portage was a half mile. Although it had rained for seven days straight, it was now bright and hot. Fred and I sat down to decide if we wanted to tote gear or just paddle back and forth for five days over the water we'd just crossed.

As we looked up the portage trail, there suddenly appeared two disheveled men and their fat wives. Obviously, they had been camping in the rain for several days and were now dragging their gear toward home. As they came nearer, groaning under their loads, Fred said to me in a very loud voice, "We can't carry all of this beer. I guess we'll have to dump it!"

One of the fat ladies started bouncing toward us and let out a little scream. "Oh, please don't do that! I'll take it. I'll take it!"

Well, of course, we didn't have any beer to begin with. I think the fat lady would have clobbered us if she hadn't been so weak from portaging.

Fred and I decided to camp at that spot for our five days. Every time we saw a party dragging their equipment toward us, Fred would pull his beer trick. It was a sight to see the canoeists drop their gear and come running. Assuming you survive, you can have a lot of fun on a canoe trip.

The Soil Is Not Deep

The dry barren dirt of Yucatan lies uncomfortably on its bed of limestone and chert. The soil is not deep or fertile. It is more suited for growing thorn bushes than crops to eat.

The Mayan natives do not have money for fertilizer. In many places, there are only pockets of soil between the *cenotes,* or sinkholes. But if you own or rent an acre or two, you can hoe it and grow enough corn for your family and some to trade in the village market on Sunday afternoons.

It is not easy to trade corn. That is what the others raise on their poor soil. Corn is the food of life. It is high in calories and the women take on the shape of beer barrels by their middle twenties. The men are hard and wiry. All of their energy is needed to fight back the thorn bush and nurse the corn until it is ripe.

During the growing season, the days are brutally hot. Even the winds that rasp across the peninsula do not bring relief. Sometimes there is no rain for long periods, and the Mayans do not know if they will have anything to eat in autumn.

The farmers go to the fields early, while there is a hint of dew and before the sun begins parching the land. It is the best time to work.

Before disturbing the earth, they prop their hoes against a tree. Then they pray to their god. They thank him for his bounty and the privilege of being able to grow a new crop. They ask his forgiveness for scratching his sacred land, but know that he will understand they must do this thing to have corn for their bellies. They do not want to scar his earth, but only chop small holes deep enough to plant seeds.

The land is sacred to the Mayans. Their lives depend on it. They are grateful that they can work it and later harvest food.

If you have traveled to other lands, you will have seen that other people see the soil as living and sacred. Usually, the more remote the rural people, the more closely they associate the soil with a deity.

Last fall, at the end of a ruffed grouse hunt, I sat on a sandstone boulder on the crest of a mountain overlooking a vast valley. I did not sit there to meditate but to get my wind back and let my Brittany spaniel rest before we hunted back to the car.

The sun had yet an hour before it crossed the circle of the horizon, and its rays splattered off the oily concrete of a superhighway. The scar wove in gentle curves as far as I could see. The Interstate was a double scar, with grass growing between, and the builders had planted more grass to keep the banks from washing. Yet, no matter how the engineers had glossed over the earth's wound with plants, it would be a scar forever.

At times, I am glad to have the massive incision there. It makes it easier to drive from one place to another. I can leave my home, wind around and catch the highway, and soon be hunting or fishing in distant territory.

If Pablo, my Mayan friend with the Spanish name, had been with me on the mountain, he would have been horrified to see the ugly scar cleaving the countryside. He would have asked, "But how will you ever heal it?"

I would have no answer for him that he could understand. "Progress" means many different things to different people.

In Yucatan there are no creeks or rivers; if the rains come, the water drains underground through the porous limestone and *cenotes*. How could I explain to Pablo, who took me hunting for ocellated turkeys, that in this country the government destroys creeks and rivers forever by stopping their flow with huge concrete dams? Pablo would say, "But if we had just one such beautiful river it would be our greatest treasure. We would always care for it so that our people could enjoy it."

If Pablo could see our delta lands, he would be surprised that we let millions of tons of rich soil wash into the oceans. Where the rivers slow and turn in deep curves, the plants act as filters to protect our bays and marine life. It would not be easy to explain to Pablo why the natural plan of nature is ruined by cutting deep channels to straighten the rivers. He would reply, "But it is such a wonderful place for ducks and fish."

There are many things that I could not explain to Pablo. So many *gringos* look at nature in a strange way, as something to be fought. The forests are to be cut, the swamps drained, the mountains carved, the prairies plowed to bedrock, and the rivers blocked. Even the air is polluted and the land littered like a coyote's den.

Pablo believes that nature is our friend. She gives us life, although sometimes she may make us work hard for it. But without her gifts we would not be here.

I am glad Pablo does not plan to visit this country. There is so much that he would not understand. I could never explain. I don't understand it myself.

Roughing It Means No Olives

In recent years, it has become popular for rugged outdoor types to go into wilderness areas to practice survival. With only minimum equipment, they learn to survive on what nature provides.

When our family goes on its annual one-week camping trip each summer, we take all of the gear we own and can borrow. It's all I can do to survive.

No family member ever quite understands who instigates these disasters. The one time my wife and I and the three kids unanimously agree on anything is when we stagger home after a week in the wilds. In unison, we repeat over and over, "Never again!"

As we were packing to leave last summer, I insisted that we take no meat. We would depend on the fish we caught each day. We would live in luxury with great platters of bass and bluegill. The first dinner in camp was a little below expectations. Have you ever seen five people fighting over the division of a half-pound bluegill?

My wife doesn't have a lot of faith in my ability to catch fish. Else, why would she have smuggled cans of tuna and salmon in her bedroll?

My wife figures you're roughing it if there are no olives for the martinis. She even brings sheets for the bedrolls.

There are a lot of definitions for a wilderness area. Anything past the suburbs is wilderness to our older daughter. Any place a boy is not likely to appear is a wilderness to our younger daughter. If there's no corner store to hang around, our boy thinks he's stranded.

When you leave concrete for asphalt, that's back country to my wife. I like to travel as far as we can on dirt roads and then pick an old logging road. When we get stuck, that's where we camp.

I like to build a big campfire at night and sing songs. The kids won't join in unless we sing a rock beat. You ought to hear us on "Tenting Tonight, Baby, Baby, Baby." And we're pretty good on "Hey, Man, It's a Long Way, Baby, to Tipperary, Baby." At least it keeps the snakes away.

I enjoy telling stories about my boyhood. That was back in the days when people knew hotdogs and hamburgers didn't grow in supermarkets. We'd go camping with one frying pan, our fishing poles, a sack of cornmeal, and a piece of canvas to use as a tent. Sometimes we'd build a lean-to. We didn't have any fancy camping gear. Anybody who took extra underwear was a sissy. We were real boys in those days and developed a lot of character.

Whenever I reach this part of the story, our son cuts in and says, "Is that the reason you kidnapped us and brought us out here? To develop character?"

"Yes, one reason. A camping trip in the wilderness teaches you self-reliance. You learn to get by without a lot of luxuries."

"Then why did you hide that box of candy in the spare-tire compartment?"

"Oh, that's strictly for emergencies."

Our boy says, "I feel an emergency coming on."

The younger daughter cuts in and asks, "Why did you bring a box of cigars?"

"In case we encounter hostile Indians. We give them tobacco and smoke together in peace."

I explained that certain things were necessities and other things were luxuries. You slept in a bedroll on the ground, and it would make you appreciate your soft bed when you got home. You took a bath in the creek, and it made you grateful for a hot shower. You had to build a fire in the morning before you had coffee. This gave you a better understanding of electric stoves. We did not always have the conveniences we take for granted today.

Our older daughter seemed much taken with this, and I could see that she was thinking hard. She asked, "Couldn't we learn all of the same things in a cheap motel?"

"But you miss the point," I said. "When we're out camping we're close to nature. We hear new sounds and also learn to appreciate silence. We smell new odors. We breathe clean air. We not only rejuvenate ourselves, but we reenact the way the pioneers and our ancestors lived. It's a link with history."

"Couldn't we get it just as well on the education channel?" the younger daughter asked.

"Forget it," my wife said. "They're only kidding you. They love it out here."

We carefully banked the fire, crawled into the tents, and got into our bedrolls. It didn't start raining until midnight.

The wind came up and the tents began to flap. As the rain poured like a waterfall, a gust of wind took down both tents. I pulled the flap over the head of my bedroll.

I heard the others scurrying about and scrambling into the station wagon. Even if I nearly drowned, I knew I'd have to wait and be the last one to seek sanctuary. Finally, soaked to the bone, I made a wild dash for the wagon.

The boy said, "I'm sure getting rejuvenated." The younger daughter said, "I feel a close link with the pioneers." The older daughter added, "I have a better appreciation of my room at home."

My wife snickered. It was our first night out. I knew it would be a long week. I wondered if I'd survive.

Old Buck and Aunt Sarah

Old Buck's legs started going out on him when he was about nine years old. Cold winds and icy lakes finally got to his joints, and it was pitiful to hear him whine at night when the arthritis stabbed him. About all I could do was try to keep his weight down and feed him aspirin when he hurt.

Buck was a golden retriever raised in our home, and I never had a better hunting partner, man or dog. He didn't have a lot of style, but he seldom lost a duck or goose.

He taught himself to swim under water after crippled diving ducks and could follow a bluebill like a hound trailing a fox. But Buck's biggest talent was understanding people. After he got to know you a little, he could figure out what you were going to do before you did it.

If I left the den to get a drink of water, he didn't pay any attention. But if I got up to make a sandwich, he followed me to the kitchen and waited hopefully.

Buck's perceptions were the reason I had to give him away. He knew two days before a duck hunt that I was going. When I set the

[45]

alarm clock for 4 A.M., he knew. And the next morning when I had to leave him because of his arthritis, it wrecked the day for both of us. I couldn't stand the pleading look in his eyes and the beseeching whines.

It got so bad that I left my gun and hunting clothes with a buddy. I'd leave home at four o'clock in the morning in a business suit, then change at my buddy's house. Buck knew I wouldn't get up that early to go to work. I didn't fool him when I left, and he sure wasn't fooled when I returned that night smelling of powder, marsh grass, waders, and duck feathers.

It took a long time to figure out where Buck should move. I had two elderly aunts across town. They were both widows and lived in a duplex with a connecting enclosed porch.

When I suggested to Aunt Sarah and Aunt Lettie that they might be lonely at times and Buck would be a lot of company, I was surprised to learn they knew some pretty salty language. They had a couple of canaries, and they didn't want a big, rough hunting dog tracking up their homes. I explained that I had Buck trimmed down to seventy pounds, he was as gentle as maple syrup, and sure wouldn't bother any dry-land canaries.

I hated myself, but I did it anyway. I told them that if they didn't take Buck we'd have to put him to sleep. They got all misty, like I knew they would, and promised to give the dog a trial.

Aunt Sarah was about 95 percent deaf, so that night I wrote out twelve pages on the care and feeding of Buck, emphasizing that no matter how much Buck pleaded he had to be kept on a strict diet for his own good. I wrote out all of his commands but, of course, I couldn't write out all of his perceptions.

The next morning I took Buck over, got him to do some tricks, and, while the sisters were competing for his affection, I left. It wasn't easy and I didn't look back.

Aunt Lettie phoned every night to let me know how the dog was doing. They had floor heat and it seemed to help Buck's joints. I thought it best to stay away and didn't drop by for several weeks.

When I rang the doorbell at Aunt Lettie's, Buck barked. He sounded like a watchdog, but when the door opened I didn't recognize him. He must have weighed a hundred and twenty-five pounds. He was almost round.

I got the two old dolls together and finally figured out what was going on. Each one was feeding him, and the cook who came each noon was giving him biscuits and gravy. In addition, Buck had learned to work all three for in-between snacks. The only trouble with Buck was that he wasn't three dogs so each could have her own.

Getting them to put Buck on a low-calorie diet was more than I could handle. I got a veterinarian friend of mine to go over and talk with them.

While Buck was slimming down, tragedy hit. Aunt Lettie had a stroke and died, and Aunt Sarah fell and broke her hip. After a lot of conferences with relatives, it was finally decided that Aunt Sarah should be moved to a rest home. By the time we got around to telling her, she was hobbling. For an eighty-year-old lady she showed plenty of spunk. She waved her cane at the delegation and said she and Buck could make it just fine, deaf or not, and nobody was moving her out of her home.

There are a lot of things that aren't fair about life. Maybe life's not supposed to be fair. The trick is to accept things and make the best of them. But once in a while you get lucky and make a good decision. It turned out that taking Buck over there was about the best thing I ever did.

Buck sensed that Aunt Sarah couldn't hear most sounds, not even the doorbell. When it rang, he'd walk over in front of her and bark and gently nudge her. She was short, and Buck's back was just the right height for her to hold on to. They'd hobble over to the front door together.

As the months went by, Aunt Sarah and Buck learned to "talk" with each other. I know a dog is limited in how many words he understands, but I don't think there's a limit on perception. Those two could communicate. He answered her need for someone to talk to, and he always listened. He also sensed that he needed her. They both gave to each other.

When Aunt Sarah went to sleep with a burner on under a pan of grease, Buck took her arm and eased her into the kitchen. In warm weather, they'd go out in the yard together, and while she planted flowers he would sit patiently beside her.

It was some team! Buck's joints eased down and they lived alone in that big duplex for seven years until he finally went to sleep forever. Not long after that, an ambulance took Aunt Sarah to a nursing home. Every time I visit her, she talks about old Buck and wonders where he is.

How to Help a Bird Dog

Although bird dogs mostly associate with hunters, the dogs seldom lie. Bird dogs are essentially truthful and when they indicate that bobwhite quail are near, it behooves the hunters to believe them.

Pointers, setters, Brittanies, German shorthairs, and other breeds which aspire to be bird dogs all have their own ways of indicating game. The most common method is to point. As game is approached and the scent becomes intense, the action of the dog speeds up. The tail wags faster, sometimes so enthusiastically that the hips are pulled along.

Varying with the individual dog and breed, the bird dog making game will put his nose closer to the ground to pick up scent or keep his head erect and try to wind the birds. The dog's entire action indicates that he is highly interested and not just pussyfooting around.

When the dog carefully works in close enough to get a hot blast of scent, he stops and points. If the dog points with style and elan, that's a bonus and gives the owner something to brag about.

At this moment, the dog has temporarily played his leading role in the outdoor drama. The remaining action is up to the hunters.

If the birds are runners, the dog must stay with them until he points or the birds tire of the game and flush. The dog also plays a role in retrieving any quail that are shot. But he does not get to play this secondary role unless the hunters do their part.

There is a great deal of time and effort involved for a dog to find a bobwhite covey or single and point it. He is not likely to lie. It goes against his training and instincts. Also, he has found that lying upsets the owner and anyone else who is along. Lying can result in disciplinary action, and the dog knows he is the one on the receiving end.

A dog that persists in lying for no good reason usually has a short career. When a dog points and indicates quail, the adrenalin in the hunters instantly reaches saturation levels. If they walk in to flush a covey but none is there, the plug is pulled from their dreams. It is a shock to their nervous systems. No hunter can survive a day of false or lying points. The repeated trauma of high hopes being dashed by bitter disappointment must come to a halt. No hunter has the constitution to permanently hunt with a lying dog. The owner finally admits that his dog might be happier with another owner in a different environment, such as being a pet to a little girl in a suburban back yard.

There are cases where a dog can justifiably lie. A feeding covey sometimes flies just before the hunters and dogs arrive. The quail scent remains warm and the dog points. A rambling covey is flushed by the arrival of a blue darter and the dogs arrive shortly afterwards and hit a hot scent. Dog owners are well aware of these circumstances and frequently use them to excuse their dogs' behavior. In fact, I have hunted where there must have been a blue darter in every tree.

Sometimes a dog points because he's a jolly good fellow. The party has hunted hard for a couple of hours and has found nothing, not even a blue darter. The dog points a stink bird or fox sparrow just to cheer up the hunters, or to get a little practice in. Maybe he wants to perk things up or simply points because it's expected of him. The dog is anxious to please his owner.

Sometimes a dog points a cotton rat. It's usually because he has not found any quail after a couple of hours and easily becomes discouraged. Maybe it's the dog's way of showing the owner that he's still trying. Fortunately, a point on a rat is not as intense as one on quail, and the owner is not fooled into becoming excited.

There are always exceptions in quail hunting, but most of the time when a dog indicates the presence of game he is giving an honest opinion. He is not deliberately lying. You must respect his judgment. If you don't believe your dog, then you should sell or give him to someone with whom you never hunt.

It is only fair that a dog owner expect truthful communication from his dog. A great deal of time and money have been spent in selective breeding, training the dog, and praying. The owner is limited in how many times he can hunt quail each season, and it is reasonable that he expect the dog to repay room and board by honestly indicating birds.

On the other hand, what might the dog fairly expect from the owner and his friends? Although the dog works cheerfully, is it not reasonable for him to have expectations? When the dog finds and points the birds, it seems equitable that the hunters do their part and knock a few down when the covey flushes.

Dogs are often disappointed by the gunners who follow them. The shooters do not carry out their roles in the drama by bringing down a bird or two.

If you have done much chasing of bobwhite quail, you will recall days when you could not hit a flushing blanket with all four corners going in different directions. And when, after repeated misses, one of the old dogs turned from his lingering point and indignantly stared at you. Under such circumstances, I have seen a variety of eyes eloquently pleading for me to get on the stick or go home and sign up for skeet lessons.

Once, after a siege of abysmal shooting, an old setter gave up on us, left the field, and returned to the truck and his dog box. I suggested to the owner that perhaps the dog was tired. He replied that the only thing the dog was tired of was our shooting. But at least he didn't cock his leg at me and try to dampen my spirits as a disgusted Brit once did.

The most upset I ever saw a dog at the inadequacy of the gunning was when a gaunt lemon and white pointer charged me after I missed on the covey flush. You could tell he was perturbed by the foam oozing out of his jaws. I think the dog might have severed my leg except that I shoved the shotgun stock between us. When a dog bites through a walnut stock, you know he's losing patience.

The owner came rushing over and wanted to know what I had done to provoke his dog. I told him I wasn't sure, but I didn't miss a bird the rest of the afternoon. I can't afford to buy a new stock every time I go bird hunting.

If I could do a survey of quail dogs, I'm sure the majority of them would agree that the most common mistake gunners make is to be out of position when a covey flushes. To a casual bystander, it looks as if the hunters don't trust the dogs.

When a dog goes on point, the best place in the world for the hunter to be, or get to with all deliberate speed, is right behind the dog. The dog has the birds!

When both hunters arrive and are just behind the dog, they should stride in together to flush the quail. The hunters should put the birds up, not the dog. If the hunters flush the birds, that's as close to them as they can get until they knock one or more to the ground. The closer you can get to flushing quail, the more time you have for shooting.

What happens to the gunner in most quail shooting is that he runs out of time. The quail either fly out of shotgun range or disappear into cover. Time equals distance in quail shooting.

When a covey of quail departs the ground, a gunner has about three seconds before the birds fly out of range, or in some cases disappear in cover so that they cannot be shot. Did the gunner run out of time after three seconds or were the quail too far? It's the same difference. Either way you had to quit firing. Time and distance are the same.

The big mistake that inexperienced hunters make is to flank out from the dog that has the quail, or for one hunter to hang back. What happens? When the birds flush, the lagging or flanking hunter has handicapped himself X number of feet, or X amount of time. He gives the quail a head start. Instead of being able to fire three shots, he gets off only two. In some cover situations, he may be able to get off only one shot.

When following singles in thick second growth, typical of much public hunting, you're sometimes lucky to get off one shot when a single scoots. If you handicap yourself by lagging behind a dog, which may only get a quick point because the bird flushes on its own, you may not get even one shot off. It's true that you will hear the bird flying off, but I have never been able to kill much by shooting at sounds. It's hard enough to hit vanishing brown blurs.

The typical hunter, new to teaming with dogs, quickly learns that something is up when a dog goes on point. He will hurry to get *almost* to the dog but then come to a grinding halt. He stops fifteen feet behind the dog and waits. The birds may be fifteen feet ahead of the dogs. The hunter waits. His partner tells him to move up but he remains rooted. The jumpy birds fly on their own. The hunter has handicapped himself thirty feet, or ten yards. He's lost about a second.

If the hunter had moved on in and kicked the birds up, he would have been able to shoot from as close to them as it was possible to get. You can't ask for any better odds than that! Instead, he lagged back and handicapped himself. He also probably made the dogs sore.

Pointing dogs are bred and trained to hold. It is the duty of the hunter to move past the dogs and flush the birds. This gives the team of dog and hunter the maximum chance against the birds. If you hunt bobwhite quail, you need all the odds you can get. Most chances at quail are earned the hard way. When you get a chance, you had better take advantage of it.

That seems a simple enough statement but it is one of the hardest things in the world to teach a new hunter. When he reaches a spot ten or fifteen feet behind a dog on point, he wants to stop. He stops so long he becomes rooted. He waits for the dog to flush the birds, although the dog has been trained that it's in his best interest to let the hunter flush the birds.

It's not always the newcomer who doesn't understand the partnership arrangement between pointing dog and hunter. Some of the old-timers flank out and dig in too. Meanwhile, the uneasy birds begin to run as the dog tiptoes behind them. When the quail finally go up, the flanker is ten or twenty yards out of position. He's earned himself some indignant dog stares, and I'm quietly hoping they'll mistake his legs for fire hydrants.

I've hunted for several years with one old codger who is kind, pays his taxes on time, and tithes. As far as I know, he is without sin or fault. However, he is a chronic lagger when the dogs go on point. He simply will not come up parallel with me so we can walk in together and flush the birds. Because he lags so far behind while I'm ahead flushing the birds, it puts me in an unsafe position. As I stride past the lead dog to flush, I try to make sure that trees in front do not block my shooting, but at the same time make sure a sizable tree is at my back to protect me from *his* shooting. The only reason I suffer through hunting with him is that he owns the land, all of it good bobwhite habitat.

Because I am usually in a more advantageous position when the birds go up, I generally have more birds than he does at hunt's end. This too worries me, for it is not advantageous to consistently outshoot the man who owns the land. Hunting invitations don't arrive in your mailbox addressed to "Occupant."

Last fall, I pleaded with the old guy to come up when the dogs pointed. I drew it out for him with pencil and paper so that he would understand. I explained that my dogs, whom he liked, preferred it that way.

On the first point, there was no doubt that the front dog had the birds and that the second was simply honoring. We quickly moved up, but twenty feet from the front dog my friend stopped and homesteaded. He would not move despite my most earnest pleadings.

I had no choice but to wade in and flush the covey. I knocked down two birds, and my friend, handicapped by distance, got off one shot but did not score.

After the dogs fetched my birds, I walked up to where he was standing and carefully unloaded my gun and leaned it against a limb inside a fallen tree lap where the dogs would not trip over it. I slowly took out a camera and photographed my friend, still rooted to his handicapped shooting spot.

"What is it about this particular spot that you could not leave it?" I asked. "Do you plan to build a monument here or perhaps drill for oil? Is it a sacred spot or is there some magnetic field holding you? Have your boots become embedded in the soil? Is there something about this spot that should be recorded for history? Does the fountain of youth flow just beneath? Are you standing in a steel trap? Just why in the hell couldn't you show respect for my dogs and come up and flush the birds they were holding?"

I knew, of course, that I had gone too far and would be asked to leave. I was pleasantly surprised when he begged my pardon and said that on the next covey he would not lag back.

A bit later the dogs went on point. We moved toward them with all due safe speed. When he was fifteen feet behind the front dog and kept going, I knew he finally understood. After that I became busy with my own affairs and paid him no notice until the shooting was over. I had two birds. My friend had none.

He was flanked out thirty feet to the side, grinning happily.

The Greatest Bass Fisherman

You might not know the name of the greatest bass fisherman in Georgia or the whole South. He's shy of certain kinds of publicity, but you may have run across him.

If you were asked to name the best angler in the South, you'd probably think of some of the famous professionals on the tournament circuit or anglers who write about themselves in outdoor magazines. But when it comes to the number of lunker and trophy bass turned into taxidermy shops, no one comes close to Billy Strayhorn. Comparing name anglers to Billy is like comparing a firecracker to a moon rocket launch. Nobody's ever shown up with as many trophy bass as Billy.

It took me five years to run him down. When I first began hearing of his exploits, I thought they were only exaggerated fish tales. As I crossed Billy's tracks from Florida to Nashville, Tennessee, I believed his catches were wispy rumors that had grown fat in the retelling. But I finally realized that Billy was a living legend, although an elusive one.

I first got wind of Billy five years ago when I stopped by a country store at Faceville on my way to fish with Jack Wingate at Lunker Lodge on Lake Seminole. When I paid for my gas, the store owner said, "Goin' fishing? Man, you shoulda been here a few minutes ago! A little scrawny fellow stopped by with the biggest string of bass I ever seen. He had a dozen and every last one of 'em weighed over ten pounds. I ain't never seen nothin' like it! I put one on the scales and it weighed 12¾ pounds!"

"Well, for gosh sakes, where did he catch them and what was he using?"

"Mister, he wasn't talkin'. He was showin'! Didn't even get his name, but his panel truck had Alabama plates."

I could hardly wait to talk to Wingate and find out if the bass had come from his camp. But Jack didn't know anything about it. During a couple of rainy spells, I visited other fish camps on Lake Seminole but no one had heard of the dream catch.

I did happen to stop by another country store and there were some old codgers sitting around. One of them said, "You oughta been here three days ago. A little runt of a man come by with four Poor-Boy coolers full of big bass. The awfullest catch I ever seen. Every dadblamed one of the fish weighed over ten pounds."

"He must have been down in Florida," I said.

"Well, wherever he'd been, that's where I'd like to be! He was proud to show them bass, but he'd clam up like a bootlegger in court when we started asking questions."

A couple of months later I stopped at a filling station at Intercession City down in Central Florida near Lake Tohopekaliga. After the kid pumping gas looked my boat over, he said, "You shoulda been here yesterday. A guy stopped by with fifteen bass and every slapdam one of them weighed more'n ten pounds."

"Was he a little sandy-haired fellow wearing blue jeans driving a panel truck with Alabama licenses?" I asked.

"Yep, that was him. You know him? Man, whatever the answer is to catching big bass, he's got it!"

I checked the docks around Lake Toho. The operators all said about the same thing. "If he'd caught them out of my camp I'd still be taking pictures."

A few months later I struck the phantom's trail at Lake Hartwell. The only difference was that this time he had a panel truck full of striped bass, most of them over eighteen pounds.

During the next three years, I stopped at so many country stores I could tell you where the Red Man chewing tobacco was kept before I went in. It was surprising how many store owners had seen the fisherman with big bass. But nobody knew his name and I was always just behind him.

I was desperate to meet him. What a great subject for a magazine article. Maybe he'd take me fishing and I could learn his technique! Two points about him had become clear. He liked to show off his fish. Secondly, he never showed them at fish camps but always at country stores or filling stations away from lakes.

It took me two more years to get the phantom's name, although I frequently crossed his trail. I left my business card at country stores all over the South. For the person who phoned me the phantom's license number, there was a $25 reward.

The call finally came through and it cost me plenty to find out who owned the truck in Birmingham. I drove to the city and for three days I did a tail job that would have been the envy of any TV detective. The phantom was Billy Strayhorn.

On the fourth morning he pulled into that country store at Faceville where I had first heard about him. I parked behind his panel truck. When he saw me striding toward him, he smiled and asked, "Wanta see a nice catch of bass?"

I looked at a dozen lunkers on ice that I knew had come from several lakes in Georgia and Florida. Billy smiled as I admired the fish and said, "It's easy when you know how."

I knew how. Billy had never caught a lunker or trophy bass in his life. He worked for Windt's Taxidermy in Birmingham and his job was driving all over the South to collect fish that anglers had left at camps to have mounted.

I got in my car and drove home. There wasn't any point in spoiling Billy's fun, even though he'd caused me a lot of sleepless nights. After all, he gave those people at the country stores a lot to talk about.

Billy just wanted to be a hero. I kind of knew how he felt. I'd like to drive up to a country store with a truck full of lunker bass and watch everybody gawk.

The Burglar

The surest way to get a limit of doves is to have a free-roaming Labrador retriever with no conscience. Regardless of who shoots a bird, the dog fetches it to you. In fact, he offers to bite any other hunter who tries to take a dove from him.

Most hunters won't leave their stands to chase a dog across a big field. You can be fairly sure they won't pepper the dog with No. 8 shot. The owner is present, and such an act could be a declaration of war.

I used to have a Brittany spaniel that was about as good a retriever as I ever saw on doves. If a bird was barely winged, that Brit would follow it a quarter of a mile. The only trouble was that he would never bring the dove to me; he'd always take it to one of the other hunters.

That little Brit never did have any faith in my shooting. I guess he'd seen me miss too many. But you would think he'd give me the benefit of the doubt once in a while—law of averages, that sort of thing.

Clyde, a hunting friend of mine, has a Labrador aptly named Burglar. He's a lousy retriever but an excellent thief. His specialty is to sneak through the bushes and steal doves from another hunter's pile.

Burglar knows this is a habit hunters other than his owner frown on. He waits until a hunter leaves his stand to walk out in a field and pick up a downed bird. Then, Burglar dives in the stack by the shooting stool, grabs two or three birds, and sneaks back to Clyde.

Burglar weighs about eighty-five pounds and has a head the size of a grizzly bear's. I've seen him fetch four doves at one time. He'll work a pile of ten doves down to one and then slink around until he finds another hunter's stand that needs unloading.

In the heat of a shooting fray, an unsuspecting hunter doesn't notice that his bag is disappearing. When there's a lull in the shooting and he pauses to count up and see how close he is to the limit, he's totally mystified. Old Burglar is so sneaky you seldom see him at work. He's as clever as an old buck at using cover and shadows.

Clyde, of course, gives the doves back, at least most of them, but not until the end of the shoot. Then the hunters, especially those who have been afield with Burglar before, all have a good laugh. But one time the Lab's thievery finally backfired, and I'm sure Burglar is the source of a story that has floated all over the country.

When the dog's work is sneakiest, Clyde accumulates a pile of doves far in excess of the daily limit. The bill came due when Clyde looked down the edge he was shooting and saw a couple of wildlife officers coming. He quickly gathered up all but ten doves and hid them in some nearby bushes.

The wildlife officers politely checked Clyde's license and shotgun to be sure it was plugged. They then counted his bag of ten doves. Everything was legal, but just as they were getting ready to go to the next stand, Burglar came out of the bushes with three doves.

This put Clyde one over the limit, but old Burglar was just getting started. As the amazed wildlife officers watched, the Lab made trip after trip until the stack had grown to twenty-five.

It was not an easy thing to explain. In fact, Clyde couldn't explain it to the satisfaction of the wildlife officers, or the magistrate in town.

Oddly enough, four or five years earlier the magistrate had been one of Burglar's victims. And, apparently, he had been waiting a long time to get even!

Evidence and defense were quickly given while Burglar, bored with the whole business, curled up and went to sleep under a table. The magistrate, with all of the dignity of his judicial position, banged his gavel and said, "I find the defendant guilty on all counts. He is hereby fined $500 for each dove in excess of twelve, a total of $6,500. In addition, his shotgun and vehicle are to be confiscated and sold at auction."

As Clyde sank slowly to his knees, the magistrate continued, "This Labrador has a past record of thievery and is a habitual offender. While there may be extenuating circumstances in the fact that the dog does not know right from wrong and does only what he has been taught, he is nevertheless a liability. I order that the dog be taken to the pound and put to sleep tomorrow."

After the wildlife officers revived Clyde, they appealed to the magistrate. They pleaded that the sentence was overly harsh. The magistrate called a five-minute recess and asked the wildlife officers to join him in his chambers. As soon as the door closed, the magistrate broke into a big laugh and explained that he only wanted to make the defendant sweat a while, that he, too, had been a victim of Burglar's acquisitive habit.

When court was reconvened, with Clyde propped up by the wildlife officers, the magistrate said, "In light of your previous clean record and the recommendation of the arresting officers, I am dismissing the earlier charges and sentence. However, the court is fining you $50 for contributing to the delinquency of a dog. This court is adjourned!"

The Hunter's Call

In recent years, it has become necessary for hunters to explain their sport to others who do not understand it, even to some who do not wish to understand it.

There are a great number of standard reasons we enjoy hunting. All of us know them and repeat them. We repeat them to each other and to people who question us about our sport.

I have thought much about it and have no new answers. After many years, I am not sure of all the reasons I hunt. It's like asking a Canada goose why he leaves James Bay in September to fly to Chesapeake Bay for the winter.

There is a season for all things. I do not have to hunt for food, companionship, to enjoy nature, or to aid conservation. But when the hunting season rolls around, I am impelled to hunt. I do not have much control over it. Perhaps none.

Hunting is what I want to do. I want to talk about it in the spring, plan for it in summer, and do it in fall and winter. It is my nature. It is a part of me, the same as my heart and blood.

Perhaps my eyes are geared to hours of sunlight like wildlife. In fall I am triggered. I have no control over it. I am like the buck that goes into rut because of declining hours of light. Or like the gobbler that is triggered into mating by the hours of increasing light.

I do not radically change in autumn when the nights begin to cool, but there are subtle changes. My wife will testify that my general attitude improves. My boss says I am more energetic. My bird dogs pay more attention to me in anticipation of glorious days just around the corner.

Old friends who have gone their separate ways for months begin to telephone. There is something mystical in the air. There is a new spring in my step. I whistle forgotten tunes when I get out of bed in the mornings. There is a feeling of being on the edge of a wonderful discovery. There is more oxygen in the air and each day is a beautiful day whether it's raining or the sun is shining. I am more alive and I can feel it in every fiber.

What triggers my internal mechanism? Is it something as simple as hours of declining light? I do not know. I only know that it happens each autumn and I have no control over its sudden appearance. Suddenly it is there and I am impelled to go hunting.

My dearest friends are those with whom I've shared a hunt. I look forward to being with them each fall and I treasure their companionship. But if there were none to hunt with me, I would still go hunting.

There is nothing more beautiful than a sunrise on a waterfowl marsh or a hidden pond in the oaks where the wood ducks whistle. I revel in the changing light and the morning is not lost if no ducks fly and no shots are fired. But I do not go to the marshes and remote ponds in spring and summer to enjoy the sunrises.

There are few things more pleasant in life than sitting around a campfire with friends on a crisp night listening to tales of victory and defeat. There is great good humor and warm companionship. But if there were no campfires, I would still go hunting.

I understand that each season hunters only take the surplus game from nature's bounty. I know that hunters pay for conservation through their purchases of licenses and taxes on their equipment. I realize that in the absence of natural predators man must crop the deer herd to keep it healthy and compatible with the forage. I am glad for these things but they are not the reason I go hunting.

My family and I enjoy wild game and we look forward to having friends share with us different foods which they otherwise might not have a chance to enjoy. Game dinners are special occasions, but I do not go hunting to make festivities possible.

I do not need a trophy for the den. I am pleased if I shoot well, but some of my most memorable trips were those when no game was sighted or shots fired.

I do not go hunting to experience dangers or thrills. Long ago I realized that most of the dangers we encounter are because of poor planning or doing something foolish to bring on needless danger.

Although one should be in good physical condition to hunt, and certain kinds of hunting are strenuous and challenging, who goes hunting simply for exercise? If one did, it would be more efficient to carry a fifty-pound barbell than an eight-pound rifle.

I do not save my money to take a hunting trip in a distant state or foreign country for different game so that I might brag about it. I enjoy telling a hunting tale as well as any hunter, but I would still make the trip if there were no one to listen when I returned.

Perhaps we go hunting for a combination of all these reasons— that these things together make the package we treasure. These are the reasons for hunting that I hear from other hunters and maybe they are true.

But perhaps I go hunting because man is a hunting animal. Did the ancient reptiles evolving from primeval seas fly because they developed wings or develop wings because they wanted to fly? Did man develop as a hunter because that was the only way he could survive or because he wanted to hunt?

It is all very mystifying and perhaps it cannot be explained. Certainly it cannot be explained to one who does not wish to know.

I breathe because my body needs oxygen. I eat because my body must have energy. I hunt because I am a hunter. These are simple things which I accept, and perhaps no explanation is possible.

On the Trail of Dog-Day Bass

Like a bird dog who has lost his nose, dog-day bass fishermen search out brush, hunt cover, and generally exhibit great style but seldom come up with a find. Let's take a look at the fisherman now, while he's handicapped, and see what really goes on during the blistering heat of summer when his quarry has the advantage.

The doldrums are a period of inactivity, listlessness, or depression. It's when the bass are not biting. This usually happens in July, August, and September when most people take their vacations.

The sensible thing to do is quit fishing during the doldrums. But who says fishermen are sensible? Fishermen go fishing when it is convenient for them, not necessarily when the fish are biting.

I am in complete sympathy with the anglers. Who wants to set a schedule for the convenience of bass?

Biologists say the metabolism of bass stays up during the hot months. The fish eat every twenty-four hours or so. It's just that they do it at odd hours and in different places, like forty feet straight down near the bottom of a reservoir.

Bass would prefer to eat right on schedule, the same as people. They change feeding times just to keep anglers guessing. The favorite time for bass to feed is when there are no fishermen on the lake.

Some bass are triggered to feed during periods of low light intensity, such as dawn and dusk. They do this just to fool anglers. When all the fishermen get trained to fishing on the dawn patrol, the bass change to midnight snacks.

When a man goes off his feed, he blames it on the boss, marital disputes, or having to do yard work on weekends. When bass go off their regular feeding period, anglers blame it on Solunar Tables, barometric pressure, water temperature, or a general malaise. That's talking in code. What they really mean is that the bass have outfoxed them again.

The bass are still in the rivers and lakes. They still eat every day. The doldrums are simply a period when fishermen get outsmarted more than usual.

There are a lot of ways we can beat the dry-runs. For instance, one can say he caught so many bass during spring and early summer that he is tired. One can state that his freezer is packed with bass fillets.

To catch bass during the summer doldrums, I try to calmly analyze the problem and arrive at a logical solution. That's why I spend a lot of time in the mountains fishing for trout.

Some outdoor writer is always discovering night fishing as an answer to the summer drought. Before trying it, the first step is some solid philosophical thinking. This means deciding how badly you want to obtain a bass.

I am not opposed to night fishing. I've done it many times and am as good as the next guy at unsnarling backlashes in the dark. Anybody I've ever fished with at night has been violently opposed to flashing a light. They claim that if you flame a cigarette lighter or use the thin ray of light from a flashlight you'll spook all the bass. No one has caught a bass for a week, but if you inhale your cigar too strongly the glowing ember will frighten all of the fish in the lake.

I'd like to know how the fish stand it when the sun comes up every morning. Do they panic when a full moon suddenly comes out from behind a dark cloud?

Last summer I was fishing with Jack Wingate on Lake Seminole about midnight when my plug got stuck in some trees. Jack wouldn't let me turn on my pencil flashlight and couldn't get the boat closer than about five feet from the dangling bushes that held the plug.

I said, "Jack, hold the boat steady, and I'll step on that log and grab the plug." I stepped out quickly and found myself balancing on a scaly log which suddenly acquired a lashing tail on one end and gaping jaws on the other. Until that very moment I had always made it a point never to upset an alligator.

I did prove that night that man can walk on water. At least, he can if he's inspired by an alligator.

A lot of things can happen while night fishing that don't have much bearing on bass. For instance, did you know that there are several species of water snakes that will hit a topwater plug? And that they all look like cottonmouth moccasins? And some of them are!

The late Omer Tyson, a fishing buddy of mine from Cairo, was casting one night on Banks Lake when he got a strike. He reared back and held on as his line stripped off. Suddenly, he noticed that the line was going straight up. He was tied into a horned owl!

He finally wore the owl down and boated it. Then he came to his senses. He had a snapping owl with two monstrous talons slinging three treble hooks. The boat was considerably overcrowded.

Omer suddenly decided that the owl wanted that plug more than he did. Omer cut the line and donated the plug to a worthy cause. The incident changed Omer's attitude toward night fishing. He said, "Any bass worth having is worth catching in daylight!"

It's difficult for me to tie a good knot at high noon. Have you ever tried to tie on a black Jitterbug on a pitch-black night when your partner wouldn't let you put on a light? It's even hard to tie a decent granny knot.

Once on a stormy night, I managed to tie an improved clinch knot in less than thirty minutes. It took just long enough to miss the bass feeding period.

Distances are confusing at night. The shoreline looks sixty yards away when you cast toward it. The plug barely leaves the rod tip before it crashes into trees on the bank. Your plug has hung a hornets' nest, but in the darkness you don't know it. You give a mighty yank and boat the nest.

Do you know what hornets do at night when they're upset? They do the same thing they do during daylight, that's what! If you land a hornets' nest, you'll be amazed at how long you can stay under water.

I've often wondered what mosquitoes fed on at night when there were no fishermen.

There are some lakes in South Georgia where it's pointless to fish with a topwater plug at night. The mosquitoes are so thick a bass is afraid to stick his head up.

Sounds are very distinctive at night on the water. You know how it sounds when someone closes the bolt on a rifle? It's a sound you instantly recognize. When your plug is hung in the brush and you give a mighty tug and the plug buries a quarter of an inch into your gunnel, there's a distinctive kuhthunk! If the plug hits you instead, there's a distinctive, "Oh, shoot!"

There are many sounds at night when you're fishing. The big bullfrogs tune up and paddyrumph across the still waters. Listen to paddyrumph long enough and it becomes "Wastin' time! Wastin' time!"

I don't mean to imply that night fishing during the summer doldrums isn't productive. It produces sore fannies, aching backs, and frayed tempers.

A few years ago, a fishing buddy of mine in North Georgia told me he had a sure way to beat the summer doldrums. The key was to start fishing Friday evening after work and keep at it until time to leave for work early Monday morning. That was back before I realized fishing was supposed to be fun, so I went with him.

By noon on Saturday, I could hardly hold my head up. I ached all over and had lost my desire to obtain a bass. My buddy was just getting warmed up. He was laughing and singing and telling me we were bound to hit a feeding period.

I finally went to sleep while retrieving the black jig I'd been bouncing off the bottom. My friend shook me awake and handed over the thermos of coffee. He also handed me a little white pill. "Here," he said, "take this Mexican aspirin."

Well, that was some aspirin! It was new, improved, reconstituted, and probably illegal. In a few minutes, I was ready to go diving and strangle a stringer of bass.

I didn't get sleepy until Tuesday. If we caught any bass, they weren't with us when we got home. I shudder to think what would have happened if he had dropped any of those Mexican aspirin overboard and the bass had eaten them. Our boat would have been torn apart by the Great Killer Bass. Needless to say, that was my last fishing trip with that particular buddy.

There is a constant rumor that lunker and trophy bass often hit at night. I myself have hooked and brought many to boat. The problem was that they lost several pounds during the fight. A one-pound bass striking a topwater plug at night on a quiet lake sounds like a monster crashing up from the deep. A two-pounder is like a surfacing submarine. Any bass that gets away is bound to be a leviathan.

There is no question that night fishing is the best way to beat the summer doldrums. When the surface water cools during the dark hours, bass move in to feed in comfort. So do the snakes, mosquitoes, and alligators.

Some anglers get so desperate during the doldrums that they will do anything to come back to the docks with a string of bass. There is one cult that will anchor over submerged trees in deep reservoirs and jig for bass in twenty or thirty feet of water. They are glorified handliners, jiggling their spoons up and down for hours. They may catch bass, but they are not bass fishermen. It's like making love by telegram or eating cheese with the cellophane wrapper left on.

It is not necessary to deny the sport of fishing to catch bass during the summer doldrums. Jerry Meyer, a field editor for *Georgia Sportsman,* told me a sure-fire method of catching bass any time. He only goes when the signs are right.

The key is being able to read the signs and put them all together. You go fishing at the exact right moment. The barometric pressure must be 29.42 two days after a cold front has passed, the water highly oxygenated from previous wind, the pH factor 6, the surface water 69° F, and the cloud cover at seven-tenths. Visibility must be less than two miles and a new moon due in three days.

When all of these factors are present at 7:20 P.M. on a Wednesday, you rush to your favorite lake. You look for a lily pad with a bullfrog sitting on it. When the bullfrog croaks, "Now's the time. Now's the time," you cast a Dalton Special at the pad, and you'll catch a lunker bass.

Jerry says he catches all of his bass this way and never heard of the summer doldrums.

Training the Outdoor Wife

Training a wife is one of the most difficult jobs an outdoorsman faces.

One reason is that he doesn't acquire her during her early formative years. By the time he meets her, she may have undesirable habit patterns so firmly ingrained that it takes great patience to teach her the correct way to do things.

The best time to start training a puppy is when it's seven weeks old. It's easy then, but if you wait until the dog is two or three years old, you can sponsor a stomach ulcer just trying to change some small detail.

A lot of wives are not biddable. Perhaps, there are some who could not have been trained properly even if their educations had started at a tender age.

When a hunter goes on an afternoon trip, his estimated time of arrival back home is probably correct within plus or minus three hours. A few hunters may need the ETA leeway increased to a week on the long side but this is far from being the norm.

One of Charley's Principles states that if a fisherman has promised to be home at 7 P.M., the fish will start hitting at the exact moment he has to leave in order to make his designated arrival time.

The same principle applies to hunting. If company is coming for an early supper, just as the hunter is starting to leave the woods he will see the biggest buck of his life. Further, the buck will disappear in an island of cover the hunter is sure he can quickly work. A lot of hunters learn to live on midnight snacks during the deer season.

It's the time factor which women can't get the hang of. They don't understand that hunting and fishing are for relaxation, and if you're on a rigid time schedule, there's no relaxation. Some wives are unreasonable about punctuality, which is what you have to do when you go to work.

For instance, a friend of mine found a deer scrape at noon. It was the first fresh one he had found all season, and he was the only hunter around. Naturally, he took a stand to wait for the buck to return, and it is totally understandable that he forgot he was to be married at 4 P.M.

When he arrived at the church at six, his bride was considerably perturbed. He explained over and over that just because you locate a fresh scrape doesn't mean the buck will show up right away. Sometimes you have to keep going back for two or three days!

He tried to calm her down by explaining that the buck had eight points. He had the buck in his car to prove it! He wanted to take her whole family out to the parking lot to see the rack but nobody seemed interested. No matter how many times he explained the logic of why he was late, she couldn't seem to grasp the point.

Anyway, the ceremony was held after they went by his apartment so he could get out of his hunting clothes and into a suit. The consensus among their friends was that the groom might have been trying to push the bride's education a little too fast.

When I leave home for an afternoon hunt, my wife always wants to know what to do about supper. Well, the last thing I'm concerned with is eating. I have enough on my mind trying to find my boots and making major decisions like what rifle to take.

In reply, I have a little song I usually sing to the tune of "I'll Be Down to Get You in a Taxi, Honey." It goes, "Leave my supper in the oven, honey. I sure do go for a half-burnt steak." I really shouldn't sing that song because it seems to infuriate her. Of course, she knew before we were married that I wasn't much of a singer.

Wives seem to think that going hunting or fishing is like going to the movies. The show starts at a certain time, and all you have to do is be there a few minutes early and you know what time you'll get out.

On a hunt last fall, I promised to be back at 7 P.M., since my wife's mother was arriving for a visit. I would have made it on time except just as I started to leave at dusk I got a shot at a four-pointer.

I'm not very handy at dressing a deer in broad daylight. I always hope that another hunter will volunteer to do it to gain woodsman experience. But I was by myself and did the best I could in the dark.

In all honesty, I did arrive home in a crimson condition. When I drove into the garage, my wife and mother-in-law came out to greet me. My mother-in-law took one look, shrieked, and ran back into the house screaming, "I always told you he'd come to a bad end!"

I knew that my wife was trying to be patient and understanding. You can always tell by the way she grinds her teeth.

"Well," she shouted, "you knew my mother was coming, and the least you could have done was shoot that deer by three o'clock."

Like I said, women just can't get the hang of this time thing. It seems like educating a wife is a life-time project.

How Fish Grow

Several months ago I had the unique experience of bass fishing with Jerry Meyer. While he was unsnarling a backlash, a bass swallowed his plastic worm.

When the fish made her first jump for freedom, it was obvious Jerry had a good one. He screamed for me to net the bass and I finally did.

I took the scales from my tackle box and weighed the flopping bass. I was happy for Jerry when I turned to him and said, "She weighs seven pounds even!"

Jerry instantly replied, "The bass weighs eight pounds!"

"No," I answered, "I checked the scales just last week. You have a seven-pound bass."

Jerry patiently explained that I had not allowed anything for shrinkage. A fish rapidly loses moisture when hauled from the water and this becomes a significant factor in determining true weight.

I told Jerry his bass had not been out of the water more than thirty seconds before I weighed her. She couldn't have dried out a pound that fast if she'd been in a washing-machine dryer.

[74]

Jerry said that I did not understand the chemistry of moisture loss. The bass had jumped three times before I netted her. On each jump, the fish was in the air long enough to have suffered dehydration, not to mention the net time. In addition, the bass had put on a three-minute battle under the water. The bass had expended considerable sudden energy and this caused drastic weight loss, plus the trauma of being hooked was bound to have resulted in bowel evacuation.

The bass was long and skinny. Jerry said she had not eaten in three days and that if she had only just fed on a school of minnows her true weight would be nine pounds. He said he was being conservative when he said the fish weighed eight pounds.

On the drive back from Lake Seminole to Albany, where I had left my car, Jerry stopped at twenty-two filling stations and bought a half-gallon of gas from each one. The attendants at each station noticed our fishing tackle.

They'd say, "You boys been fishing?"

Jerry would reply, "Yup."

"Catch anything?"

That's when Jerry would jump out, open the back of the station wagon, and take the lid off the ice chest. "I caught the big one!"

"What's it weigh?"

"A little under ten pounds."

I've often wondered how much that fish grew on Jerry's long drive to his home in Talking Rock, North Georgia. For all I know, by now it may have beaten George Perry's world record bass caught in 1932.

Fish biologists say that a largemouth bass does pretty well to grow one pound a year in a lake of average fertility. Under unusual conditions, a bass may gain two pounds or so in a year.

I think the biologists need to consult with Jerry Meyer. He showed me how a bass could grow a pound a minute.

Bass don't stop growing after they are dead. In fact, that may be their period of most rapid growth.

I've learned a lot from Jerry and other technical experts. They don't measure by the metric or the American system. They have their own: Two fish equal a stringer, five fish equal a big stringer, and seven ounces equal a pound.

For a number of years it was a constant source of embarrassment to me that as an outdoor writer I had never caught a trophy bass, one weighing ten pounds or more. I had seen several anglers who had achieved this, and actually touched one of them, but it had never happened to me. In the tradition of all true Southerners, I went out one night and changed my luck. The next day I caught a largemouth which weighed 11¼ pounds.

I am sure she weighed this much because I tested her on four sets of scales. On the first three, she weighed 11 even, but I did not mind driving the twenty miles until I found a set where she pulled 11¼ pounds.

I did not allow anything for shrinkage, one reason being that the two buddies with me did not believe the theory. They did admit the bass was long and lanky and if she had been fat and full of eggs she would have weighed considerably more.

Since my wife had always wanted a stuffed bass for our living room, I had the fish mounted. When it came back from the taxidermist, the long, skinny fish had turned into a stocky one with a sagging belly, obviously one which weighed twelve or thirteen pounds in the raw.

Unfortunately, at my request, the taxidermist had installed a bronze nameplate stating where the fish had been caught, the date, and weight. I hung the fish in a dark part of the living room where an admirer could not get in reading range of the plate without leaning across a table studded with broken bottles.

Whenever an unexpected visitor, such as the paperboy, came to our home, I would take him into the living room and modestly point at the bass. No matter who the visitor, even the garbage collector, he would always ask how much the fish weighed.

I was always totally honest and would reply, "A little under twelve pounds."

The trouble was that some of the admirers would notice the plate and edge around and read the 11¼ pounds. I decided to remove the plate. The trouble was that it left a mark, as though the mount had been tampered with.

When I had the bass transferred to a new wooden mount, with no plate giving away the weight, my bass both gained and lost weight, depending on the visitor. The trick was to get the visitor to say what the largest bass he ever caught weighed before he asked me how much my mounted one weighed.

If his largest bass weighed ten pounds, mine weighed 10¼. If another said his record bass was twelve pounds, mine was 12¼. The most my bass has ever weighed is 15½ pounds. I never beat their records by more than one-quarter of a pound. It's one thing to be flexible, but I don't believe in lying!

My Friend the Tree

At the crest of Bearpen Gap there is an ancient hemlock tree, its scaly bark scarred by wounds from old lightning thrusts. The tree has overlooked Glory Valley for three or four hundred years, silently reviewing the changing troops of Indian braves, British redcoats, and tough Scotch and Irish settlers.

The tree is decaying and does not have many years to live. When it was young, its roots drove deep into fractured bedrock, expanding so powerfully they shattered the granite. The tree has always had a solid grip on life.

The hemlock and I have been friends for fifty years. The cold mountain rains have washed the soil from some of the massive roots on the downslope side. My favorite lap is the one where I snuggle between two roots, forearms resting on them like a rocking chair. I can clearly watch the jagged deer trail and scan the shadows for careful bucks.

In the whole mountain range, there is no tree as large as my friend. One crisp morning before the sun whisked the fog from the gap's shoulders, I asked the hemlock why he was the only mature tree rising high above the second growth.

When there was no reply for several minutes, I looked up the scraggly trunk, blotched with resin, and saw for the first time that the grain was twisted and deformed. It is strange how you can know someone for so long but never really see him, like waking some morning to find that your wife's eyes are gray when you thought they were blue.

He said that if I could climb his massive trunk I would see two Shawnee arrowheads, plus crude gashes from flint axes and keener ones from pioneer blades. Many times he had almost been roasted alive as wildfire spread through the dry autumn leaves, whipped by wandering fall winds.

I can hardly remember a season when I did not kill a buck coming through the gap. I go there each fall and wait. Sometimes I must wait all day and keep coming back for three or four weeks, but I have learned patience from the hemlock.

He will not help me, although I know that he sees and hears the ghostly bucks slinking just off the trail behind the does. He is an impartial observer, favoring neither the hunter nor the hunted.

One afternoon he told me the deer had used that same gap for three hundred years that he remembered. In the old days, when all of the trees were mature, there were not many deer, the leafy canopy shading out browse. But after a wildfire, the sunlight would bathe the ground and new growth would spring from the black dirt. The deer would drift in and the does become larger and healthier, giving birth to twins and sometimes triplets.

The hemlock has great wisdom for he has seen many things. He knows the deer numbers run in cycles. Where there is lush browse, lavish mast crops, and the blueberries are thick in August, next spring there will be many fawns to nibble the wild flowers. In other years, food will be scarce and the deer will wander away and the skinny does become barren. The hemlock does not worry, for he knows the rhythm will change and some fall there will be more and stronger bucks fighting for the fat females.

My friend, with his many years, does not look at time as you and I. He knows that nothing is permanent, that some day even the massive mountains will be whittled down to mere hills and finally to monotonous coastal plains. And even that will change when the earth's crust is thrust upward again, the thick layers of sedimentary rock folding and twisting to make new mountains.

The hemlock does not dwell long on such thoughts. He says it is better to live one day at a time, neither dwelling in the past nor worrying about the future. Each day is a new birth. Every morning is a new adventure.

Perhaps you think a tree does not have much to do. If so, you have never met my friend. He has many duties besides greeting the sun or dark clouds each dawn. He must stand proudly, a monument of permanence to those who need such things. He is a lighthouse, a marker to guide woodsmen, and a resting place for ravens and warblers. His roots must cling to the soil to hold him erect and to prevent the water from stealing his dirt. The new roots must expand and probe deeper for nourishment.

He must give off fresh odors and make music with the wind, from the soft rustle of needles to the snap of dead branches cracking from a sudden relentless gust. All of these things he must do, but most of all he must survive.

He has to survive the droughts, the deep snows, the clinging icicles trying to strip his needles, searing wildfire leaping to catch a strangle hold, and tiny insects sneaking beneath his bark to bore out his innards.

I have rested against his comfortable trunk for so many seasons, and he has told me these things. He does not complain of bad times, for they are the nature of life. They only cause one to enjoy more the good times. He has them each day, for he sees many new things and he understands them. What he likes most of all is to calmly survey his countryside, observe each change, and know that he is a part of it all. It is important to have a feeling of belonging, to understand his relationship to the whole.

Sometimes I worry about my friend. Far up his trunk, there is a spreading brown spot, rotting from tunneling insects and chipped away by woodpeckers. Perhaps underneath I am worrying about myself. I do not know how many more hunting seasons I will be able to climb the rocky trail to nestle with my friend and watch for bucks.

There is not much I can do for my friend. Each fall, along with my rifle and pack, I carry a trenching shovel and a sack of fertilizer. I throw fresh soil over the newly exposed roots. Above my friend, I dig a trench and pour in the nourishment, mixing it with humus so that it will not be too strong for his system. I cover the half-circle with black dirt and chips of stone, knowing the rains will carry the food to the roots.

When I have done all I can, I load my rifle, sit down, and prop against my friend. Sooner or later, a careless buck will come up the ancient trail. It does not matter when. My friend and I always have a wonderful time.

The Truth About
My Fear of Cactus

Something totally inexplicable often happens on hunting trips. For instance, the one I recently made to Mexico. The fertile plains of the states of Sonora and Sinaloa, between the Gulf of California and the towering Sierra Madre Occidental Mountains, offer some of the best wing shooting in the world. Great flocks of mourning doves, whitewings, and waterfowl winter there.

For several years, I had wanted to hunt the elegant quail and collect a pair for my den. My old hunting companion, Stretch Jensen, and I finally saved enough money and made arrangements to hunt out of Navojoa, south of Ciudad Obregon.

Just as we were departing, my wife said, "Isn't it wonderful? The Senior Flower Society is taking a bus tour through Mexico and will be passing through Navojoa. Zelda Hightower is leading the tour and I asked her to stop by your Fiesta Motel." Well, Zelda is the worst gossip in our section of the state and I'd as soon bump into a scorpion. But Stretch and I forgot about it, figuring if she stopped we'd be out hunting.

We had made a great deal of preparation for the trip and read everything we could find. Between us we must have learned twenty Spanish words and phrases. We took no dogs, either pointers or retrievers, because every wild plant has some sort of thorn on it. For our protection, we had leather chaps.

But as happens on so many trips to a strange place, we were not totally prepared when we arrived in Navojoa last winter. There is no way one could be ready for Ixcuintla, our guide, a Yaqui Indian from the wild mountains who knew about as much English as we did Spanish. We soon changed his name to Cartuchos because his chief function seemed to be scrounging shells from us for his ancient double.

Cartuchos kept us from getting lost and got us back to the motel each night. The first two days we were covered up with mourning doves and whitewings. But Cartuchos's main ambition in life was to increase the gross national consumption of tequila.

For the third day, I showed him a color plate of an elegant quail. He grinned and said, "*Mucho!*" We drove past the farming plains into the edge of the desert. Cartuchos pointed to the sparse vegetation, all of it prickly with stickems, and said, "*Peligroso!*" (Danger!) He wore sandals and the native cotton knee-length britches and a light shirt. Stretch and I wore boots and chaps.

Quail in arid country do not hold, as long as they remain together as a covey unit. The trick is to flush and scatter them and then they'll hold tight as singles. We spent the day chasing valley and Gambel's quail before spotting a covey of elegant quail hiding in cactus shadows. After scattering them, I walked up a pair and got a double, a male and female. I had the trophies I had come to Mexico for.

In my excitement, I backed into a cholla, fanny first. If you are not familiar with cholla, it is an instrument of the devil. Hundreds of small barbed fish hooks, so small you can hardly see them, break off into anything that brushes against them. They cling to the flesh, migrate deeper, and fester.

After I quit jumping around, Cartuchos said, "*Vamos al Fiesta Motel. Mucho problema.*" I knew it was a problem, all right, about 300 darts burrowing into my behind. The only way I could ride was to sprawl out on my stomach across the hood.

It was dark when we reached the motel, and I told Cartuchos,

"Call the doctor. *Llame al doctor, por favor* and *por Dios!*" Cartuchos, like all people south of the border, loves an accident or crisis. Waving his arms, he yelled, "*Dinero por medicina!*" Stretch handed him a wad of bills and in a few minutes Cartuchos was back with the medicine—four bottles of tequila.

By that time, I had my clothes off and was stretched naked across the bed on my stomach. Stretch said, "It looks like you were shot in the butt with a load of No. 12 rat shot. But I can't see anything to grab hold of and pull out."

We did not possess the most important equipment for any hunting trip to Mexico, a magnifying glass and a pair of tweezers.

In the excitement, a bottle of tequila was quickly emptied. I drank it as a painkiller, Stretch as a relaxant, and Cartuchos because it was there. The motel owner said the doctor was out of town.

Cartuchos suddenly had an idea. He grabbed Stretch and explained that he was going to find a nurse, an *enfermera*. They were back in about half an hour with four of them, magnifying glass, tweezers, and all.

They were strangely dressed for nurses. Two wore bikinis, one a robe with nothing under it, and the fourth looked like a grape being squeezed out of a G-string. Cartuchos had obtained help from the local cat house! But at that point, I didn't care. I would have welcomed succor from *El Diablo* himself.

From the squeals of delight, I gathered it was a picnic for them. To be more comfortable, they loosened what few garments they wore and went to work, pulling cholla spines one at a time. It was a game. *Una por Carlotta. Dos por Rubia. Una por Maria. Dos por Carmelita.* A tequila sunrise for Cartuchos.

When they had extracted about *veinte y cinco* (twenty-five) with about *trescientos* (three hundred) to go, the others left. It would be a long night, but apparently a hilarious one for the nurses. I wished I knew more Spanish so that I could understand their excited jabbering.

There was a knock on the door. I turned my head and yelled, "Come in and join the party." Zelda Hightower opened the door with a delegation of the Senior Flower Society behind her. For about *un momento* there was only deadly silence. Then Zelda screamed, "Sex fiend!"

Try explaining that one to your wife when you get home from a hunting trip.

Before the Saints Come Marching In

My old friend Frank Hill phones two or three times a year. He usually has a message that cheers me up. Even if I'm feeling good, Frank makes me feel better.

Although we have been hunting and fishing buddies for a quarter of a century, Frank calls me by my last name. I have never asked him why. He looks at things from a different angle than other people.

When I answered the phone one night recently, it was Frank. I had not heard from him in five or six months but he didn't start off with salutations or weather reports. He said, "Dickey, have you ever known any dead people who hunted?"

While my mind was trying to get out of low gear, Frank said, "Well, I never knew any that hunted."

I had never really given the matter a lot of consideration. Most of my thoughts in that direction had been to wonder if bird dogs went to Heaven. I had gotten far enough with the idea to know that there were certain bird dogs that did not deserve to go to Heaven. In fact, if they made it, then it wouldn't be Heaven.

"Dickey," Frank cut in on my rambling thoughts, "I used not to know hardly any dead people. Now it seems the older I get the more dead people I know. In fact, I know more dead people than I do live people."

I knew Frank was trying to get somewhere, so I didn't interrupt his meandering.

He continued, "If all those people are dead, and not a single one is hunting, and one of these days I'm going to be dead, that means I won't be doing any hunting."

I grunted. There was no argument with that line of reasoning.

"You know what that means, Dickey? It means I better do a lot more hunting than I've been doing."

I gulped a little on that. I could remember when Frank hunted six days a week and would have gone on Sundays except that he firmly believed there was a divine reason for resting on the seventh.

"Dickey," he said, "you know what I've just done? I've retired! I just can't put up any longer with work getting in the way of my hunting."

Now, that shocked me. I had been under the impression that Frank had retired years ago. I knew that from time to time he got new projects going, such as a doe scent that would make bucks come to you on the gallop. At times he prospected in the mountains for gems and dug for hidden money around abandoned farmhouses. Off and on for forty years, he had experimented with artificial lures in an attempt to design one that would make a bass bite when the bass didn't want to.

It was as natural for Frank to have a project going as for a hound dog to board a family of fleas. But I thought he had given up serious work as bad medicine a long time ago.

I knew Frank didn't expect any comment from me when he began playing his harmonica. He works on four or five new pieces each year, and after months of practice any one is suitable for running bobcats out of the county. His latest medley included "Faded Love," "Alabama Jubilee," and "Old Dogs and Watermelon Wine." I'm glad he's a lot safer with a shotgun than a mouth harp.

After the serenade, Frank said, "Dickey, you come by here on the tenth and we'll shoot some of those little dove birds."

I looked at the calendar over my telephone. The tenth was on Wednesday. "Frank," I said, "thanks just the same but I can't make it. I still have to work for a living and ..."

Frank cut in, "We'll shoot four afternoons. There's a big milo field with a pond right in the middle. You remember it."

I said, "I'd like to come, but it's four hundred miles and right at the busy time of the month."

Frank didn't seem to be paying any attention to what I was saying. "I'll give you that easy stand by the old dead walnut tree."

"Look, Frank, there's just no way I can make it. Maybe later."

He didn't hear me and kept right on talking. "I got a young Brittany that catches those shot doves before they hit the ground."

"Frank, I'm sorry. I just can't make it."

He said, "You ain't been listening to me. How many dead hunters you know who're going to be hunting doves this season?" Then he hung up.

Well, Frank sure knows how to ruin a guy's sleep. I tossed and turned for an hour thinking about all of my old buddies who can't shoot doves anymore. You can't swing a shotgun when there's six feet of clay on top of you. I got out of bed, found my checkbook, and sat down to do some figuring.

I tumbled back into bed and thought of all the ways I could juggle my work schedule. The boss was already pretty jumpy about the number of days I had taken off. He said I was the only person he ever heard of who had had six operations for appendicitis. There was simply no reasonable way for me to make the trip. But I kept thinking about what Frank had said. I didn't know any dead hunters who were still hunting.

The worst thing that could happen would be getting fired. I got up and went to the telephone and dialed Frank and woke him up. I said, "Frank, I changed my mind. I'll be there."

"Thought you would," Frank said. Then he took his harmonica and said, "Now we're going to have a little 'Saints.' The full title is, *'Before* the Saints Come Marching In.'"

On the Antlers of a Dilemma

The trouble with hunting deer is that there seems to be an unlimited number of ways of not quite bagging one. If being close counted, I'd be in all of the record books.

No one knows how to cook a close.

One thing every hunter can do is sit down after the season and review his errors so he won't make them again. The worst mistake is one we've made before or many times.

As for new errors, I'm not sure what we can do about them. Just when I think I've already made all of the known mistakes, a new one pops up.

For instance, this past season I was stop-and-go hunting in a slow drizzle hoping to see a slinking buck or to push one from his bed in the thick cedars. My variable scope was on $2 \times$ so I'd have a wide field of view. In order to keep the lens dry, I had cut a wide rubber band from a truck tire inner tube. The band tightly covered the fore and aft lenses. When the scope was needed in a hurry, all I had to do was flip the rubber band off. I know that's the way it works because one of my hunting buddies who's good with gadgets told me so.

On this particular afternoon, I sneaked quietly along the forest floor on wet pine needles and leaves. I'd walk a few feet, pause, and search the openings and edges ahead of me. As a matter of fact, I was doing a pretty good job of playing Indian scout because suddenly ahead of me I saw a huge buck sparring with a sapling.

With one glance it was obvious the buck had more than his share of tines. He was only forty yards ahead of me, unaware of danger, and I was already deciding where the head would look best in my den. I slowly raised the rifle and began to remove the rubber band from my scope.

I must have been more excited than I thought. The rubber band slipped from the forward lens and catapulted into my master eye with several hundred foot-pounds of energy. I have no scientific data on the ballistics of rubber bands at one foot but the remaining energy was sufficient for me to think I'd somehow shot myself.

I can't recall if I yelled or screamed, but I do remember the buck looking in my direction to see what was disturbing the silence. If I'd had the presence of mind to fire the rifle left-handed, I would have had plenty of time for an easy shot, perhaps even pointing like a shotgun by looking over the scope. But I was too busy shouting uncomplimentary remarks at my absent hunting buddy who told me about the rubber band as a protective lens device. I think the buck finally strolled off. How do you explain back at camp that a deer gave you a black eye?

It's not a mistake I'm likely to make again. If worst comes to worst, I'll use the lens caps that came with the scope.

Scopes and scope mounts are subject to periodic creep, thus providing another potential alibi for missing a deer. You can zero the sights from a bench rest so that you're shooting groups the size of a quarter at a hundred yards. Everything is coordinated. You can then gently put the rifle down, post an overnight guard on it, and fire it the next morning. With five cartridges fired, three will group about the size of a washtub. There will be no trace of the other bullets, both having vanished somewhere in outer space.

If you carefully analyze the situation, you'll find the conditions of the second day were exactly the same as the first. No one touched the rifle or scope between tests. The only thing that could have put the scope out of alignment was a pair of mating houseflies vibrating the mounts. While that might seem impossible to a shotgunner, it is perfectly reasonable to a rifle shooter. Unbelievable things happen all the time when you're trying to keep a barrel coordinated with a telescopic sight.

You never know what to expect from the union of a scope to a rifle. Last season, before an elk hunt, I had considerable trouble sighting in a 7-mm Magnum rifle at two hundred yards. I finally had to settle for a basketball group since my plane was leaving in an hour.

Once seated in the plane, I was treated to the spectacle of the cased rifle falling from the top of a luggage conveyor and bouncing off the concrete ramp. The airline did not charge extra for the performance. It's a bonus thrill for flying commercially. I shuddered and, despite three changes of planes, did not look toward another conveyor until I reached my destination after dark.

Two hours before daylight the next morning, I was hanging onto a horse going up a mountain side too steep for a lizard. There had been no time or daylight for sighting in my rifle. It was now jammed into a scabbard and I watched it bounce and jiggle, hoping that if the horse fell on that side the scabbard might block my leg from breakage.

For five mornings, we rose before dawn, raced through the mountains, and returned to base camp after dark. There was never time to stop and sight in the rifle. I did not see an elk on the trip, possibly because the guide was training his horses for a marathon.

The only time I took the rifle out of the scabbard was to see if I *could,* in the event we saw an elk and the guide would stop. Even then, I managed to drop it and watch the rifle carom down a talus slope.

When I returned home, I decided to test-fire the rifle from a bench at two hundred yards on the local range. I cushioned the fore-end and butt with sandbags and fired five rounds. Fortunately, two friends were watching because no one would believe I could fire a group the size of a dime at two hundred yards, especially me.

The shake, rattle, and rolling the rifle and scope had suffered on my scenic tour had jarred them into perfect harmony. I could have fooled with them on the range all fall and never gotten them as well synchronized. Creep can work two ways. However, you can't depend on its going the correct way very often. I sold my rifle and scope right on the spot.

When somebody asks me how often to check the sight alignment of a scoped rifle, I give him a standard answer—it can creep out at any second. If it's in alignment, don't touch anything. Breathe softly. No one understands creep.

A hunter saves himself a lot of grief if he can learn from the mistakes of others. That's another reason a review session is valuable during the off-season. You don't have to make all of the mistakes, but let other hunters make some. Generals know they can't anticipate everything. That's the reason they have maneuvers.

That's why I'm willing to share a mistake I made in Mississippi a few years back. It might prevent you from doing the same thing.

The weather had turned warm, but the rut was on and the bucks were moving in daylight. I'd found a fresh line of scrapes and one set of tracks looked as if they were made by an elk rather than a whitetail. Well before daylight, I arrived at the spot I had chosen to sit. With my back against a big pine tree, I could look up and down an old logging trail with good visibility in case the big buck checked his scrapes.

Shortly before sunrise, I heard a couple of bucks locking horns along the edge of a soybean field. They were snorting and grunting and I could hear their hooves churning up the surface as they dug in to push. I figured the winner would be the buck that had made the scrapes. Although the fighting bucks sounded no more than seventy-five yards away, I didn't think I could ease through the brush for a shot without spooking them or spectator does and lesser bucks.

I decided to wait where I was, and it turned out that I guessed right. In the meantime, it was a long wait and the sun came up and started warming things. Suddenly I heard a buck down the logging road sparring with branches. I turned around and got ready to shoot.

That's when a four-foot blacksnake came wiggling out of an old log. He was moving slowly, probably looking for a sunny spot to warm up in. The snake crawled up almost between my legs and then stopped and coiled. I must have moved because he began to rattle his tail in the dry leaves. Blacksnakes do this to imitate real rattlers and bluff people to leave them alone.

Well, I could hear that buck coming near, crunching dry leaves and raking his head at every branch in reach. I knew that if the snake didn't quit rattling, the buck would spot him and then me. That vibrating tail sounded like a sewing machine in the brittle leaves.

I had to do something so I took a chance the approaching buck wouldn't see me and I reached out and grabbed the blacksnake right behind the head. He wasn't at all happy about it and began to whip and thrash his tail around. So I had to put my rifle down and grab the tail.

My plan had been to throw the blacksnake as far as I could, but his agitation changed that. He'd just make a lot of noise and maybe alert my buck and spook him. I decided that the best place to put the snake was in the game bag of my old coat so I headed him in and he did the rest. It was just the sort of warm spot he wanted in the first place.

The snake calmed down. I guess he liked the warmth from my back and went to sleep. I picked my rifle up and waited for the buck to come on up the trail. Suddenly I saw a gray shadow rounding the turn in the logging road and I got all set to shoot. The buck hit a patch of sunlight and I quickly checked the antlers, what there was of them. It was a little fork buck, feeling his oats, no doubt inspired by all the fighting and breeding going on around him.

The buck came on toward me, suddenly got a whiff of a scrape and eased carefully into the small opening to check it. My problem was not to be seen, heard, or smelled, and hope the buck would leave quietly, with no loud whistling alarm cry that would alert every deer for half a mile.

I watched the little buck put his nose down almost in the scrape and get a strong whiff of urine the big buck had posted. The fork jumped back and looked around. For what seemed like five minutes, he peered into the second growth. Satisfied the scrape owner was not coming, he deliberately walked to the scrape, hunched over it, and quickly drenched it. Then, after checking for safety, he scampered away like a teen-ager who had pulled a joke on teacher.

I still thought it was a good bet to wait for the big buck, especially if he hit the trail of the younger buck approaching his scrapes. I settled in for a long wait, maybe even dozed.

I was alerted by a steady crashing sound. The big buck was not coming down the logging road but busting through the brush to his scrapes. I eased my rifle up and waited, my finger on the safety ready to move it once I got a good look at the buck. He sounded like a bulldozer as he plowed his way through the scrub and came closer and closer.

There was a loud crash of brush no more than forty feet away, and then silence. I couldn't believe it. The buck, with a rack like a dried-out Christmas tree, was standing broadside to me. I pushed the safety off as I moved the scope dot to his neck and gently began to squeeze the trigger.

At that instant, I felt something crawling up my spine. *Rattlesnake!* electrified my mind and I jumped! You may not think it possible to broad-jump fifteen feet from a sitting position with your knees tucked up. If so, you've never been in my situation. At some place during the jump, I pulled the trigger and was peppered by falling pine cones from above. I had shot straight up. I have not seen that big buck since.

Several weeks later, when I could calmly review the incident, I realized I had made one vital mistake, which I shall never make again: Don't ever forget that you've put a snake in your hunting coat!

Last fall I made another error I don't intend to let happen again. My pickup truck was in the shop for repairs and I borrowed my wife's old Volkswagen for a local late-afternoon hunt.

The weather had been dry for two or three weeks and I was able to drive the little car well back into the woods. I left the car and walked about two hundred yards to a winter wheat field to watch for bucks during the last hour of daylight.

For a long time nothing came but the cold. When the light had dwindled until the scope could barely collect enough for me to see, a six-point buck strolled into the field. I quickly aimed for a high neck shot and the buck collapsed. I walked over, poked the buck with my rifle, and went back to get the Volkswagen.

When I returned to the edge of the field, I was faced with the problem of loading the buck, fortunately not a large one, into the rear of the passenger compartment. After considerable grunting and straining, I got him inside. It would have lightened him to field-dress him but I didn't want to mess up my wife's car.

As I turned into my driveway, there was a sudden loud commotion in the rear. I stopped the car and turned back in time to see the buck unraveling and then thrusting his antlers into the front seat space to my right.

The buck was considerably irritated. I could tell by the way he was grunting and kicking. In fact, he was about as sore as any buck I ever saw. It was obvious he did not like his current location and was about to change it to the front seat.

I realized that would be overcrowding things, and I made an instant decision to give him my space. I hit the brake, bailed out, and slammed the door.

The buck was no happier with all of the space. I realized he was cutting the interior, so I reached for my hunting knife. Then it dawned on me that if I did manage to reach in and cut the buck's throat, it might mess up the car beyond recall.

My rifle was on the floorboard in the back seat, no doubt with the sight alignment creeping. I ran inside my house and grabbed another rifle and a handful of cartridges. My wife followed me out and, I must say, added to the confusion by screaming for me not to shoot any holes in her car.

It was a good point, and I suddenly realized I couldn't shoot the buck inside or leave him there, either. We live in a suburban tract and the noise was beginning to attract attention.

I knew something had to be done so I stood by with my rifle while my wife swung the driver's door open. The buck sprang out and never looked back. I raised my rifle to fire but then realized it was against the law to shoot in the suburbs. Also, it was unsafe. On top of that, I didn't want word getting around that I was hunting deer in the suburbs. And several other things.

The buck must have been only grazed and stunned. I stayed up listening to radio and television news to see if there were reports of an upset buck in the suburbs at our end of town. There were none, and nothing in the morning newspaper, so I guess the buck made it back to the woods.

The whole affair is another mistake I'll never make again. From now on, I'll drive my pickup truck hunting or not go. If a deer comes to in a pickup, he won't need any help to get out and there's no way he'll damage the vehicle.

The Linoleum Two-Step

Hypothermia is a hazard to outdoorsmen, and just recently discovered by outdoor writers. It's when the body temperature becomes so much lower than normal that all of your sins start passing before your eyes. If your body temperature stays low too long, you won't have any time left for additional sins.

Hypothermia has been around all of the time. It's an illness usually associated with well diggers in Alaska or brass monkeys. Most deer hunters north of the Rio Grande have experienced tinges of it which they paradoxically call being "colder than hell."

Since bits of the illness are uncomfortable and large pieces can be fatal, it would be reasonable to expect hunters to take precautions, especially at camp, where they spend most of their time. But if you think hunters are necessarily reasonable and logical beings, you haven't been around many of them.

For instance, take the floor coverings at deer camps. Do you know what kind of floor covering holds cold longer than any other? If you don't, you've never spent the night at a typical deer camp.

It's linoleum! That's what it is, linoleum, the universal covering for all camp flooring.

Linoleum is ten to twenty degrees colder than the air outside. When you step barefooted on it, your whole body temperature drops. Stand on it long enough and you'll surely expire from hypothermia.

Linoleum is the reason no bucks are ever killed near camp. The screams from people whose bare feet come in contact with it keep the deer scared off.

There are several reasons for covering a floor with linoleum. None are justifiable.

It is inexpensive and forgiving. You can spill a lot of strange concoctions on linoleum, but a little soap and water quickly erases all traces, even those from vermouth or squashed olives.

Also, the skin peeled off bare feet doesn't stick permanently.

You would think that hunting shacks would have warm throwrugs of deer hide or old camouflage jackets. A hunter rolling out before dawn could put his feet on something warm.

No deer camp has such luxuries. When your feet swing out, they hit linoleum! It's like being jolted with electricity. The cold instantly goes through your body, and the top of your head feels like the skull is peeling off.

The hunters who build deer cabins must consider it sissy to leave pure planking. I'd even prefer a dirt floor, soil not being near as icy as linoleum.

Of course, it does help wake one up! I've seen some strange dances at five o'clock in the morning.

Laura Coleman is always complaining that her husband can't dance. Well, she ought to see old John at camp when he's doing the Linoleum Two-Step or the Linoleum Hop. The Linoleum Hop is kind of like a Sioux war dance, except when John does it he spends nine-tenths of the time in the air and one-tenth with his feet touching the linoleum.

Even if you sleep with woolen socks on, it doesn't help much. You have to put your feet on the floor in order to get your britches on. Wool doesn't stop the laser beams of cold from the linoleum floor!

Bunks in deer camps are never built near the fireplace, light switches, or lanterns. If you're the first to wake, you have to cross the room to turn on the light or poke the coals.

When hunters set the alarm clock the night before, they deliberately place it across the room from the bunks. When it rings a few minutes later, someone has to get up, hit the cold linoleum, dance across the room, and slap the clock off.

If you want to see some sound sleepers, just look at a room full of deer hunters while the alarm winds down. It isn't that no one hears the alarm. Everyone is waiting to see who will weaken first, get up, and put his feet on the linoleum.

By the third day of camp, I'm always afraid someone will shoot the clock from his bed. That's why no deer camp will allow guns to be stored near bunks.

One logical solution to the problem would be for hunters to take sheep-lined bedroom slippers to camp. But that must be considered sissy, because I have never seen it done.

A grizzled old hunter told me there was a definite purpose for flooring with linoleum. Once your bare feet hit it before dawn, that's the most you'll suffer all day. Even if you fall in an icy creek, it will seem warm.

There is no doubt that linoleum teaches you to withstand hardship. First of all, you try to learn never to think about it. It's a Spartan type of mental and physical training.

If you begin worrying about the absolute zero of linoleum before going to bed, you will no sooner get warm under the covers than you will have an overwhelming urge to go to the bathroom. The bathroom is always outside, but first you have to cross several miles of linoleum.

So you lie there awake all night suffering from the choice of three options, none of which is pleasant. You have the choice of getting up and going, lying there awake all night, or the third option, which is unthinkable at your age.

It's no wonder so many hunters go to sleep on deer stands at daybreak!

I have learned a lot from going to deer camps floored with linoleum. Now, when the alarm clock goes off, I can lie flat on my back with legs extended toward the ceiling and put on thermal underwear pants, slip on my britches, put on two pairs of wool socks, and then a pair of thermal boots without losing my position. I may be late for the morning hunt, but I start the day off with warm feet.

What Is a Shotgun?

My *American Heritage Dictionary* defines a shotgun as "a shoulder-held firearm that fires multiple pellets through a smooth bore." That's it! That's all it says.

I like that definition, but a lot of my friends would not. To them, it leaves too much unsaid. There is no mention of fancy walnut stocks, inlaying, and admiration for the patient craftsmanship that goes into a fine gun. There is no heart or sentiment, no hint of happy days afield.

People look at shotguns in different ways. The finest shotguns I've ever seen are owned by collectors who don't shoot them. They just like to look at shotguns, and have friends admire and envy them.

Some of my hunting friends tote around rusty shotguns with the original bluing represented only by a few scaly freckles. The only time the thirsty steel gets any oil is when the gun is knocked over where a leaky automobile just parked. To them, a shotgun is a tool made of wood and steel. Nothing more.

To my wife, all shotguns look the same. She could go through a shotgun show and each piece would seem identical to all the others.

She does not understand why I need a new shotgun when there are a dozen in the house now. As far as she's concerned, I could go quail hunting with a .243 rifle.

I know shooters so attached to their shotguns that I suspect they sleep with them. A collector friend of mine got married not long ago and took four shotguns on his honeymoon. He didn't want to go hunting. He simply wanted to have the guns handy so he could take them out of their plush cases and fondle them.

An acquaintance of mine bugged me for two years to visit his home and see his fourteen-year-old boy's shotguns. I finally went over and was surprised to see that the boy had one shotgun for every year of his life. He was proud of them and it was obvious that this ownership was the most important thing in his life. It was all I could do to cough up a few compliments. Every one of those shotguns was a standard field gun with not a single distinctive quality. It was like looking at any small-town hardware store's gun rack.

Pride in ownership is a strange compulsion which I don't understand, but I know it's pervasive and I accept it. You yourself will recall many incidents when hunters bragged of their shotguns, even gun number 458,679 in a lot run of 500,000 over a period of time. Every gun which came off that assembly line was identical to the others, but not to the owner of 458,679.

To many people, a shotgun is a personal thing. I have a friend who has a shotgun mounted in a convenient place in his bathroom. Every time he goes in there and sits down the gun is nice and handy in case he wants to rub it.

I'm not critical of people who enshrine shotguns as personal objects of admiration and worship. In fact, I'm usually more fascinated by them than their firearms. They were preceded by a long line of kings, emperors, shieks, generals, and common man.

However, from the practical standpoint of using a shotgun to hunt, I'd like to get back to the dictionary's definition of a shotgun. It's a tool for projecting shot at a target, usually a flying bird, clay target, or small mammal.

A firearm is basically a simple thing. It's unique in all of the world in that it produces the largest reward for the least amount of effort, pulling the trigger.

Anyone with the strength to overcome a three-pound trigger pull can set the contraption off. It takes almost no effort, but the reward is immediate, a loud explosion and projectiles sent on their way to overcome distance and hit something. The shotgun is a fascinating mechanical device with great power which attracts small boys like a magnet, and men and women of all ages.

It is a marvelous contrivance, but it has its limitations. Used mostly for hitting moving targets, it's no better than the shooter who pulls the trigger. It has no radar and can't overcome human error. For a given target, a thirty-dollar secondhand shotgun has the inherent capability of an English double costing $5,000 or more.

Each has a wooden stock so the shooter can mount the gun to his shoulder and eye. Each has a barrel, a hollow tube for guiding the shot. Each has a mechanical gimmick for firing the shell. Each has a trigger so the shooter controls the firing. Whether the target is hit or missed depends on the person who holds the shotgun and fires it.

The shotgun enables an accurate user to reduce to possession a departing bird or a squirrel high on a limb. It's a tool that makes it possible for him to overcome distance and speed. The hunter can't scamper up a tree and catch a squirrel or run fast enough to nab a quail on the wing. The tool adds to his power.

A shotgun is a compromise. Power is given, but only limited power consistent with certain boundaries of sportsmanship. Choke, gauge, and shell selection define the limits at which game can be killed cleanly. If the hunter is too close when he shoots, such as at a sitting rabbit, he destroys the meat which the hunter's code prescribes that he eat. If the game is too far when the trigger is pulled, the hunter wastes a shell, or much worse, he cripples his quarry.

The power of decision is given only to the hunter, not to the shotgun. A firearm is an inanimate object, with built-in powers and limitations, and cannot exercise judgment. Only the user has this capability.

A shotgun is a compromise in another way. It's not selected for a particular shot in the field, but for shots expected to occur most of the time, a sort of rough average. An improved-cylinder choke for bobwhite quail is not chosen because its optimum pattern is twenty to twenty-five yards. It's selected because most quail are killed between fifteen and thirty yards. Within these distances, the user expects to shoot at most quail he flushes. He might kill a quail at ten yards without tearing the meat to pieces and he can kill a bird at thirty-five yards, but for most shots on a given day he expects to shoot at distances between fifteen and thirty yards. The shotgun, or choke, is a compromise on what happens most of the time.

The sportsman selects his shotgun to be fair to the species he intends to hunt. He is neither over-gunned nor under-gunned.

A shotgun is a marvelous instrument, and some have great beauty. But they are not as beautiful as the hunter who knows and understands his shotgun and exercises keen judgment in its use. The shotgun expert, with his powers of instant decision and coordination, is a symphony of grace in action.

His power and art are greater than that of the instrument he uses.

That Night Before

It was 3 o'clock in the morning, and I had been wrecking the bed for five hours trying to grab some sleep. In another two hours it would be time to get up and open the duck season. Warm milk, a hot shower, or Chinese relaxing exercises hadn't helped. Sleep continued to elude me as I rooted around on the mattress trying to find a hole where I could stick my head.

The bed next to mine had groaned and creaked for several hours. Out of the darkness Bob Fuller asked, "How many have you killed so far?"

I was surprised that he was awake too, but I knew exactly what he meant. "According to the latest count, I've bagged a hundred and forty-seven pintails, a hundred and twenty-one mallards, and scores of teal. Haven't missed a shot. How many have you gotten?"

Bob struggled up, lit a cigarette, and said, "You're ahead of me on sprig, but I'm way out in front on mallards, even though I've been taking only the drakes. My best shooting was a triple on honkers."

"That's strange. I didn't see any Canadas."

"You must be on a different frequency," Bob replied.

Further conversation revealed that all our shots had been taken at a minimum of forty yards, that most of them were doubles and triples, and that the scene had been in Technicolor. There was some argument over whose dog had done the better retrieving.

Finally Bob threw off the covers and said, "Let's go get some coffee."

"We might as well. We aren't going to get any sleep."

At the all-night cafe we sat sipping black coffee, but the caffeine was like a tranquilizer after five hours of overworking my adrenalin glands on flight after flight of imaginary ducks. We were amazed at the number of bleary-eyed hunters who kept drifting in, long before time to go to the blinds. "Maybe those guys couldn't sleep either," Bob said.

He took another pull at the coffee, leaned forward, and in a confiding tone said that he could never sleep the night before a hunting or fishing trip. His statement was as welcome as a long-lost bird dog. All my life I have been afflicted with the same kind of insomnia, and for years was ashamed of it. I even went to the extreme of faking sleep in camp while I lay in torment for hours.

My affliction simply did not make sense. Here I was, a grown man fortunate enough to have enjoyed a variety of hunting and fishing in many areas, but anticipation of even a routine trip threw me into a torment of wakefulness. A mere bluegill fishing trip was enough to destroy sleep. I'd pass the long hours in fantasies of myself cleverly outwitting the fish, making them strike my secret lures when no one else could get a strike, and landing dozens of monster bluegills. My fishing skill was invariably shades above Izaak Walton's.

Desperately I tried various methods of overcoming the insomnia. Two nights before a trip I would deliberately confine my sleep to three hours, on the theory that the next night I'd be so tired and drowsy that I couldn't avoid a long, blissful sleep. It didn't work. My fantasies simply became more outrageous; I got triple after triple on coveys of bobwhite quail.

Naturally, all this played hob with my coordination. In the cold light of midmorning, when fatigue had set in, I would shoot horribly. Quite often the shots I missed were the same ones I'd handled so easily the night before.

My hunting companions were not reluctant to mention that I needed an unusually large number of shells to bag a limit of bobs. And though I had the perfect alibi—I was tired and sleepy—I didn't dare reveal it. The idea of a grown man not being able to sleep because he was going hunting would have thrown them into hysterical laughter. Or so I thought.

Of course, we all remember how our first boyhood trips were preceded by excitement and inability to sleep. I remember the Christmas when I got my first .410 single-barrel—and my father's promise to take me rabbit hunting the next morning. With the gun lying by my bed I tried to sleep, and finally did drift off. Suddenly I awakened, rushed into my dad's room, shook him, and asked if it was time to go. He switched on the bedside lamp and looked at the clock. "Midnight is a little early for rabbits," he laughed. For years I've wondered if he was really asleep or just lying there counting cottontails.

When I reached my thirties I was still suffering from this secret childhood disease, and some prolonged reading in psychology didn't help. I decided that I was emotionally immature or subconsciously rebelling at the idea of growing up. I probably didn't hate my parents, or anything as complex as that, but something seemed to be missing from my makeup.

Anyway, I went for a physical examination. Beyond telling me that my stomach protruded, which my belt buckle revealed as bluntly, the doctor pronounced me in good condition. I was hesitant to tell him my basic problem, but after all he was my family physician, so I cautiously broached the subject. After sympathetic encouragement, I gave him the whole history. He smiled knowingly and gently. "It's merely a mental block that you've built up over the years," he said. "A remedy, but not a cure, will be some mild sleeping pills."

He wrote out a prescription and, as I was leaving, asked, "When are you going hunting again?"

"Why, I'm going up to a deer camp for the opening this weekend."

"Do you have room for another hunter?"

"Sure, Doc. But I didn't know *you* hunted."

He leaned back, stretched his arms over his head, and said dreamily, "It's been a long time—since I was a kid. But I'd like to go. I assume there are no telephones?"

"Of course not. I'll have an extra rifle for you and pick you up Friday afternoon."

After a big dinner of steak and hash-brown potatoes, Doc said, "Take one of your pills and we'll turn in soon. I don't want to get started in the card game with the others."

We hit the sack at nine and I immediately began shooting whitetails. In fact, for the next hour I shot so many ten-point bucks that my shoulder was aching. I turned on the bedlamp, sheepishly glanced at my shoulder in the mirror, and said, "Doc, that pill ain't working."

"Well, take another one and try to relax. Think of something restful."

I stumbled back into the rumpled blankets and tried to concentrate on isolated South Sea islands, with the wind gently fluttering the palms and the sound of distant native music in cadence with the waves washing up onto a crystalline beach. I took a deep breath and sighed as the soft light of a full moon bathed the island. And then, from a distant clump of palms, a huge whitetail walked majestically out onto the naked beach, shook his great antlers and stamped around in a challenge. The answering herd of bucks sure looked crazy swimming around in the Pacific surf!

Doc seemed to be doing a lot of turning and twisting. I got up again. "How many of those pills is it safe to take?" I asked.

Doc was awake. "One more and that's all."

I went back to hunting whitetails. When I grew weary of stalking to within ten feet of them, I began shooting from a stand. Next I started measuring all the racks I intended to enter in the Boone and Crockett record competition.

Doc's restlessness made it difficult for me to get accurate measurements of the trophy antlers. Finally he swung out of bed and fumbled for the light. "Where are those sleeping pills?" he asked.

I tossed him the bottle. "Doc, you look like you've been delivering triplets to a sow bear. You've got to learn to relax!"

He mumbled something about the intelligence of deer-hunting patients and went back to tearing up his sack.

About two in the morning we both gave up on the sleeping pills. As the card game was breaking up, Doc and I went in and made coffee and began the long wait for hunting time.

I reached my forties still suffering from the night-before disease. But psychology was making great strides, so I went to see a headshrinker whom I knew casually as a hunter. I outlined my problem and offered to take him quail hunting as payment for each consultation. The psychologist jumped at the opportunity. He gave me some blocks to shuffle around, then a square-peg and round-hole test, and assessed my I.Q. He then spent forty-five minutes telling me what a great hunter and fisherman he was. Sleeping the night before a hunt never bothered *him*!

The following Friday I met him at a motel near Greenfield, California, for a Saturday-morning hunt. We shared a room. I thought the large leather bag he carried had shotshells, but it was filled with bottles of gin and vermouth. The psychologist made a good dent in them before dinner, and by bedtime he was pretty well stoned. Mumbling something about Freud and the sex life of quail, he dropped off into a snoring sleep. He had taken so much juniper anesthetic that I could have dug out his appendix with a barlow knife without worrying about waking him.

I didn't get much sleep that night, but I felt better than my learned pal the next morning. We found covey after covey but he couldn't have hit the quail if they'd been buzzards. That ended my projected series of consultations. I can do without hangovers; and besides I could do those block tricks better than he could.

After a while it began to dawn on me that perhaps I was not unique. Many others might be afflicted too. If so, we could get together and start an "Insomniacs Anonymous" organization. I thought back through the years. There were the fishermen who would pick me up two hours before it was necessary to leave, the duck hunters who insisted on being in the blinds long before shooting time, the bobwhite gunners who hit the fields at daybreak, though they knew the birds wouldn't move until the dew began to dry. I recalled the guys who never went to bed at all, but stayed up all night in bull sessions.

It wasn't easy, but I began to ask others if they had ever experienced sportsman's insomnia. One of the first I questioned said, "Listen, I got to where I could sleep in a foxhole on Guadalcanal right through an air raid. But if I'm going pheasant hunting the next morning, I *never* drop off into a real sleep!"

To my amazement and pleasure I found that I had company everywhere, even among men who had hunted in Africa and India. Thoughts of a ruffed grouse on the morrow still made them toss all night long.

The man who really solved the problem for me was C. T. Buckman of Visalia, California. Buck, now passed away, had hunted all his life, but was always as eager as a kid on his first time afield. Even on a fairly routine hunt, where a field was loaded with doves and Buck knew he would limit out, he showed up full of anticipation. Each hunt was a joyful new adventure to him.

Driving back from a dove shoot one evening, I told Buck about my sleepless nights. He smiled and said, "The same thing still happens to me. Don't ever let it worry you. The time to start worrying is when you *don't* have that spark that keeps you awake."

Of course, Buck was right. I should have realized it years ago. For most of us, anticipation is really an incurable disease. Incidentally, the most doves I ever got at night without missing a shot was three hundred and sixty-two. I could have bagged more, but it was only four hours to shooting time, so I got up and put the coffee on.

How's That Again?

There are a lot of otherwise sane people who become mumblers when they go hunting or fishing. They are quite talkative when outdoors, but their volume drops to a low hum. I'm positive they're trying to communicate, but I never know about what.

It doesn't matter how many times I plead with them to speak up, they keep mumbling. I know they're not talking to themselves because they frequently turn to me with a quizzical expression. They expect an answer. Although I haven't understood a word they've whispered, I've learned to smile and nod in agreement. If their expression demands it, I can shrug like a Frenchman. This usually gets me by.

On the other hand, it can get you the reputation of being the town idiot. For instance, last year I was in the stern of a duck boat with a 25-horsepower motor on the way to the blinds. The mumbler in the bow turned his head partly toward me and slurred some lip movements. I smiled and nodded.

It was not quite daylight, but the visibility was good. I kept a straight course down the channel I knew so well. The bow mumbler accelerated his muted conversation and finally turned all the way toward me. He looked at me pleadingly and mumbled something.

I cupped my hands and shouted, "What the hell is it?"

He mumbled some more. I shrugged my shoulders, smiled, and said, "*C'est la vie.*"

At that instant, I became very occupied. We smashed amidship a huge log that was partly submerged in the middle of the channel. The motor shaft broke, and the cowling went sailing over the bow. I found myself holding the top half of a motor in my lap, the flywheel still turning.

My companion's fall had been cushioned by a bag of decoys. It was the first time I knew he could talk loudly. In fact, he was screaming, "Blip, blip it, I told you there was a log in the channel!"

It's true that if one engages in certain outdoor activities his hearing is affected. It's cumulative. The hair-like hearing receptors are gradually worn down by outboard motors, chain saws, four-wheel-drives, shotguns, upset wives, and other noisemakers. I've been around such items a great deal and do not mind admitting that part of my hearing is missing.

In fact, I'm anxious for all outdoor companions to know it. I'm not deaf but simply can't hear mumblers. Rather, I can hear the mumbling but can't distinguish the words. If there is a competing noise, such as a 50-horsepower motor, I can see the mumbler's lips moving, but I can't understand the words. If I'm operating the motor from the stern seat, only a couple of feet from the motor, you'd think the mumbler would have enough sense to increase his volume.

He doesn't. No matter how many times you ask him to speak up, he continues to mumble. One winter day I was running the boat back to the dock. Most of the morning had been spent silently waiting for ducks that never came. My buddy hadn't said two words.

But once we started for the marina, he began to mumble. I cupped my hands and shouted, "I can't hear you over the motor!"

He replied, "Mumble, mumble, mumble."

I cut the motor and stopped. "What'd you say? I can't hear you with the motor running."

"What'd you stop for? I was just wondering where the ducks are."

I cranked the motor, and as the boat planed, I could see the mumbling start up again. I cut the motor and said, "If you expect a reply to your muttering, you'll have to make it louder. Don't you understand that I'm sitting on the motor and can't hear above it?"

I started the motor, but before I could get the boat on the steps, he began mumbling. I shut the motor off, and we went through the whole thing again. In fact, I cut the motor thirty-three times before we made it back to the dock.

A week later, I found out that he'd told it all over town that I was the worst boat operator in the state and dangerous to ride with. I couldn't go a hundred yards without cutting the motor.

It's hard to believe how many mumblers there are. Last summer I paddled a canoe around a pond while a buddy cast a popping bug for bream. It was dead calm and silent. You know how sound travels on water? Well, he was such a low-decibel mumbler that I couldn't make out a word he was saying. When he made a bad cast, I tried to look encouraging. When he caught a bream, I smiled. He mumbled for two straight hours. I finally found out what he was trying to say. There was a slow leak in the canoe.

A couple of years ago, I went duck hunting on Lake Seminole with David Morris, editor of *Georgia Sportsman*. As we settled into a two-man blind after putting the decoys out, I said, "David, why don't you call the shots?"

A small flock of ringnecks headed our way, and I waited for David. Apparently, he judged them out of range, because I didn't hear him say anything. Suddenly, he stood up and knocked down two ducks. As we paddled out to pick them up, I said, "David, could you call the shots a little louder? Like 'Get ready' and 'Now'?"

A flight of scaup scooted in high and began to circle. Knowing how well scaup will decoy, I figured David was going to let them circle closer. I didn't hear a word, but suddenly David was erect and firing. One of the scaup plopped in among the decoys.

A pair of wood ducks started in, and I looked at David's lips to see when I should stand up to shoot. Well, he's the worst mumbler I've ever seen. His lips didn't even move, but there he was, standing up and scaring those woodies off.

I asked David if I could call the shooting on the next ducks that came in. He said all right. When a bunch finally came in, I stood up, shot three times, and then yelled, "Get ready, David, here they come!"

The Gun-Starers

Within the shooting fraternity—those who enjoy shooting a rifle, handgun, or shotgun at a target or animal—there is a strange breed known as gun-starers. Most of us at one time or another are afflicted with the malady.

A gun-starer is a person who, when he misses a clay pigeon or bird on the wing, holds his gun out in front of himself and glares at it. Some may not stare for more than a few seconds but others may stare for a full two minutes. No word is spoken nor is there any profanity or screaming to relieve inner tension. The shooter who erred simply holds the gun and stares at it.

What does he expect to see? It's the same gun he's used for fifteen years, the same grouse shotgun that hangs in his den for nine months a year without so much as a glance to see if specks of rust have freckled the bluing. He'll walk by the shotgun several times a day as it stretches ornamentally among his den trophies. He may relax in his easy chair directly under the gun each night, but he never really looks at it.

He feels the presence of the gun and is vaguely aware of it resting peacefully between hunting seasons but he never stops and studies it. The gun is an old and trusted friend, a constant. It doesn't change. There is no reason to pause and look at the gun. But if the gun were removed by his wife, he would instantly realize it the second he walked into the den.

As the early dove season approaches, one August afternoon he will take the gun down for a practice session at the skeet field with some old hunting friends. At station one, he breaks the singles and chips the doubles.

When it's his turn at station two, he calls for the high-house bird and shoots three feet behind it. He's made this shot smoothly and effortlessly hundreds of times before. In fact, it's one of his favorite stations. But this warm afternoon he misses in front of his four companions. They are all standing behind and each is fully aware that he never caught up with the target, much less followed through with his swing.

The shooter holds the gun at an extended port arms and glares at it. He doesn't consciously study the barrel, stock, receiver, or trigger. He just stares at the gun.

He loads the old friend for his option high-house, his first miss, and takes the shot again. This time it's only two feet behind the clay disc. The gun is immediately extended at arm's length and he glares again. Perhaps this time he turns the gun and looks at the other side. Then he shakes his head, loads the gun, and breaks the low-house bird.

Obviously there's nothing mechanically wrong with the shotgun. It still has the capability of powdering a fragile target. Nothing on the gun has been changed during its nine-month vacation. The choke has not been reamed nor the stock adjusted. The wife has orders not to touch it, not even for dusting. The most damaging thing that could have happened was a spider crawling along the matted rib.

At station four, a tough one with full deflection, the shooter misses both the high- and low-house birds. He remains at the station, slowly turning his head from side to side in utter disbelief.

It's another's turn to shoot but he does not leave the station. He stares at his gun.

Why does he stand there staring at the mechanical contraption in amazement? Why, of course, he is silently communicating with his four friends. He is sending out body signals pleading for a sympathetic word. With his actions he's implying to the four witnesses that it could not be his fault. Something is wrong with the shotgun.

He hasn't discovered what's wrong with the gun but the whole world must understand the misses are the fault of the gun. Perhaps if he stares long enough at the gun a part will drop off, the reason for missing will become obvious to his companions, and his pride will be saved.

Old Charley must restrain himself at times like this when he's on the receiving end of a heart-rending signal pleading for a kind word of sympathy. My natural inclination is to tell the sufferer if he'll quit staring at his gun and lead hell out of those targets he can get out of the dramatics business. His performance is not convincing and his audience of four has grown weary with the stench of green ham.

Old Charley wants to ask, "Did your barrel get bent when you took it out of the case?" or "Here, let me see if the tang has melted and the stock has a six-inch drop!" I'm almost compelled to ask if he's gotten some new gold inlay on that worn-out gun and is he staring to see if it's as pretty as he thought it'd be. Maybe if the gun needs all that admiration the whole squad should quit, go back to the clubhouse, and all stare at the gun together. Make an afternoon of it.

But old Charley sometimes keeps his mouth shut, even when it hurts. I hate to lose friends. The wounded ego of a shooter nursing pent-up anger at himself is as dangerous as a wounded lioness in tall grass. He is looking for emotional release, namely the first guy who taunts him or pricks his raw pride.

The frustrated shooter needs encouragement and compassion. If you've ever done much shooting, you know! You've been there yourself. It's no different from every aspect of life. Who doesn't need a kind word, friendly encouragement, or a compliment every day of his life?

One day the shooter will learn to admit his mistakes and not try to blame them on something else. He will be a better person when it happens. When you're honest it's a little easier to live with yourself. It's also easier on those around you.

As for releasing the bottled-up frustration and anger when you miss, most shooters quickly learn the formula. They simply say, "Aw, shucks!" or a reasonable facsimile. That does the trick every time.

The Wild Life at Lake Bountiful

There are certain laws that govern fishing. For instance, if your boss asks you to work one weekend a year, it will be the weekend when the fish hit anything dropped in the water. If you are fated to be sick during spring, it will be the opening week of the trout season. No one knows how these laws got started or who's to blame. The laws are simply a part of the way things work. Like, if it's going to rain for a solid week, that's when you take your kids camping.

There is no book to read to help you plan ahead to protect yourself from governing laws. Things simply happen under a given set of circumstances. For instance, no one ever forgets to put the plug in his boat when he launches at a vacant ramp; he only forgets when there's a big crowd around.

Last summer my wife insisted on spending a day fishing with me. She wanted to see what I found interesting at five o'clock in the morning. I had told her about the thrill of the changing colors of the sunrise on a lake, the sight and sounds of wildlife, etc.

I selected a fish camp not too far away, and we drove there in the afternoon. Right off I suspected that things were not going to go well. I've been fishing out of that camp for fifteen years, but that was the first time I had ever seen a sorority party held there.

When we went over to the lodge for dinner, I started to introduce my wife to Mabel, one of the most efficient fish-camp waitresses around. Mabel, who stacks up like a Shetland pony, threw her arms around me and squealed, "Still trying to get a bite, huh?"

I honestly don't know what got into Mabel. She's young enough to be my daughter, maybe granddaughter. That's the only time she's ever hugged me.

Later that night, the sorority girls became a bit loud. In fact, two of them knocked on our door and asked us to join the party. I politely declined, explaining that we were going fishing early and needed our sleep.

They said they were going fishing, too, but they would sleep when they got back home. It seems they were having some sort of fishing tournament to raise money for a school function. I told them that was nice and practically slammed the door in their faces.

My wife had not said a word. Then she started to unload. "I can see why you have such a good time when the fish aren't biting. Now I know what you mean about all of the 'wild life' on the lake. No wonder you have so much fun communing with nature."

There didn't seem to be any point in trying to explain. I knew I'd just mire in deeper. In fifteen years of fishing from that camp, that was the first time I'd ever seen an unescorted female.

I had a lot of trouble sleeping that night. The girls belonged to some religious cult, and they marched around the cottages chanting, "Zummm." Over and over they kept chanting, "Zummm. Zummm." My wife was pretty restless, and I asked her if we should join the chanting. It sounded soothing and might relax her.

My suggestion was not a good idea. But it got even worse when we left our cottage to go to breakfast a little before daylight. As we took a shortcut across the lawn, we saw a couple of girls transfixed in meditation. They were also stark naked!

One was sitting, and the other was standing on her head. My wife gasped, "Well, I never!"

To calm my wife, I said, "They're just hippies, but remember that they have the right to practice their religious beliefs."

My wife burned her lips gulping down black coffee. I kept telling her how beautiful it would be on the lake when we finally got away by ourselves and could watch the birds. With any luck at all, we'd see a lot of shore and wading birds.

"Yeah," she scowled, "I know what kind of bird watching you've been doing."

We were running late by the time we got back to the room, grabbed our gear, and walked to the dock. There were six or seven girls running around. All of their clothes together weren't enough for one.

My wife growled, "What's the uniform of the day here? Strings?"

I rushed her into our boat and was about to crank up when one of the sorority girls ran over and asked sweetly, "Can you help me? My motor won't start."

My wife said, "No wonder. You ran it all night. It's tired!"

I went over to the girl's boat and climbed in, with her right behind. I checked the fuel connection, the choke, and pressure. The girl was bending over me, watching every move. I whispered, "Please don't lean any farther. You're busting out all over." Then I yanked the starter cord, and the motor kicked off.

I forgot all about fishing and took my wife to Lost Creek. Nobody goes up there anymore, and I figured we would be away from all traffic. A light wind was building as I cut the motor and we drifted into a quiet area. Then I heard two peaceful voices chanting, "Zummm. Zummm." I looked toward a sandy cove and found that two meditators had changed location but still hadn't found their clothes.

That's the last trip I've made to Lake Bountiful. It was my wife's idea for me not to go back. I've quit trying to explain what happened on that trip. The governing law is that some things can't be explained and the more you try, the deeper your foot goes.

Losing Another Crop

Hurrying through the darkness of the huge oak and beech trees along the Tombigbee River in Alabama, my partner headed inland toward an ancient longleaf pine. It was easy following the deer trails that wound through the thick wire grass.

Jason stopped at the huge pine and leaned his old Model 97 hammer shotgun against the scraggly bark. It was early spring and the chill in my shoulders had not warmed from the two-mile walk. Or perhaps it was the tingling hope that I might get a shot at Old Zeb, the terrible gobbler who ruled the territory, lord and master of a dozen hens and scourge of young toms or older males who dared to flirt with one of his harem.

Jason whispered, "You go north half a mile and I'll go south and we'll meet back here at noon. Well, I guess I'll lose another crop this year." He moved off softly in his light boots and I took a fix off the Big Dipper and poked along, knowing it was more than an hour before it'd be light enough for a turkey to open an eye.

Strange people, those Alabama turkey hunters. Totally obsessed with outwitting a particular gobbler each spring, not just some stray tom with a two-inch beard. A peculiar madness comes over these hunters each spring. They are as powerless under its spell as the gobbler propelled by his glands to perpetuate the species.

Having hunted with Jason for several years, after a first dubious acceptance, I was sympathetic regarding his compulsion but I could not fully understand it. Eleven months of the year, he stayed close to home, avoided trouble with John Law, and seldom even took a nip. But I knew what he meant when he said, "I guess I'll lose another crop this year."

Planting time unfortunately arrives during the spring gobbler season. If you stay out in the woods for thirty days, you don't get any planting done and there's no harvest in the fall. I knew Jason had lost crops the past two years trying to get a shot at Old Zeb, and it was a mystery to me how he kept his rickety farm from being taken over by the bank. Before Old Zeb, there had been three crops lost on Good Jelly and, come to think of it, I can't remember if Jason has ever planted a crop. There didn't seem to be much hope for him because when you knock off what an Alabama turkey hunter calls a *terrible turkey,* the czar of the empire, another immediately takes his place, after whipping all the ambitious claimants.

If you haven't hunted turkeys much, you may think they all sound alike. They did to me the first few years. But not to Tombigbee hunters. They get to know the old boys so well they give them names. They can tell a gobbling two-year-old before he gets his wattles shaking good. One old male will have a baritone cluck-cluck, another a whisky gravel, and another a different accent. One of the biggest ever shot was a high tenor, and, of course, they had a special name for him.

As the false dawn sneaked in, I found a couple of big logs and poked around to see if anything rattled. It was a good place to hide and call, with visibility at ground level in nearly every direction. I loaded up and scrooched down to wait. It'd still be an hour or more before Old Zeb or another turkey would fly down and start gobbling.

I couldn't get my mind off Jason. He was hunting during planting time again, the wife and the kids short of money and the roof leaking, and all Jason had on his mind was Old Zeb. It wouldn't make any difference if he shot Old Zeb because he'd still lay out in the woods and talk to those turkeys until he found out who the new king would be. He'd just hang around the different turkey camps, maybe call up a gobbler for a kid to shoot, or barbecue a pig.

I didn't see how his wife held the family together. Jason was around the farm most of the time but he managed to miss planting every spring. On a farm, you have to grow something besides kids. Thinking of Jason and his hunting, I had to smile. If I told him at noon somebody was sleeping with his wife, he'd say, "You drive right over there and tell that man I'm going to shoot the hell out of him—after the turkey season."

Jason has his own turkey-hunting code. I don't know where it came from but it's the same for a lot of those crazy Alabama hunters. They won't pull a trigger unless a turkey comes within forty yards and some have a code that the turkey must be tricked to within twenty-five yards. They see no sport in shooting a turkey at a hundred and fifty or two hundred yards with a scoped rifle. Anybody can call a turkey that close, or stumble into one.

The challenge is calling one to within forty yards or less. In fact, some of the old-timers never pull a trigger anymore. When a big gobbler comes strutting in with blazing blue head and wattles on fire, the wings whomping and big feet stamping, not caring if he finds a hen to love or a gobbler to fight, the hunter stands up and hollers, "Gotcha!" The startled king gapes an instant in surprise, lets out an unmistakable putt-putt alarm, and races off on those long legs, squirting white as all the fight goes out of him.

Jason has never accepted invitations to visit my home in Memphis, and we see each other only during the spring turkey season. Four or five times a year, when I'm practicing on my mouth yelper, I phone him long distance, if his phone isn't cut off. I don't say "hello" or anything, just start the conversation with my best impression of an urgent hen pleading for a gobbler, a sort of purring cluck.

Jason laughs and says, "You're getting close. Another five years and you'll be mated." I know he's reaching for his padded cardboard box where he keeps his call, a tiny horseshoe of lead with a rubber membrane stretched across it. He says, "You need a little more flirty in it, as though you're a hen come real proud." Then he gives just the right sexy call over the phone.

Sometimes we talk turkey for an hour or two, giving lost chick calls, rally calls, and the whole works, even blasting each other with gobbles. When my phone bill has all I can stand, I give the putt-putt alarm and hang up. It makes me feel better for days just talking to Jason.

As the sun peeked over the trees, I kept trying to figure him out. He's a normal family man all year until the spring season gets close. Then he undergoes some chemical change, like maybe he has moon fever. The family wakes up one morning and he's gone—for a month.

There was a big flompy noise in the pine ahead of me and a young tom came flying down. He landed with neck stretched out, and a hen glided down behind him. He wasn't twenty yards away and I could see he was a two-year-old, with a beard hardly more than a kid's first peach fuzz.

I didn't really have my mind on turkey shooting. The more I thought about Jason, the more I wondered about him. Why did those old turkeys get to him so bad? Why had he developed that personal code where he'd hunt for just one gobbler, as if he held a grudge against him? As far as I knew, Jason had come from a normal home and parents, with no other sign of insanity in the family.

Over the years, I've tried to draw Jason out about his affliction but about all I ever got out of him was that spring gobbler hunting is worse than dope.

When the sun began pouring straight down, I wondered how Jason was doing. I heard a gobbler way off to the south, but no shotgun. I picked up my gun and loafed back to the meeting pine. Jason was sitting there.

He looked up and said, "I saw Old Zeb this morning. He worked real good to about a hundred yards. Then he got sneaky, circled around as quiet as a chicken thief, and came in through some brush to about fifty yards."

"You could have nailed him."

"Yeah, but he wasn't in forty yards."

Jason picked up his gun and I followed him back to the camp.

When we came in sight of the old shack, I decided to forget the couch bit. I'd better accept Jason the way he was and the way he'd always be. It simply would never *occur* to him to stay home and plant when the gobbler season was open. He was an Alabama turkey hunter, not a city man living his days out in quiet desperation.

First Aid for Joggers

It takes all of the inner discipline I can summon not to join the joggers who come jouncing down our street. Many of them are outdoorsmen conditioning themselves for hunting and fishing trips.

They are a friendly lot and always wave in a desperate sort of way. I'm sure they want to make friends. Misery loves company. Besides, they never know when a part will fail and they'll need someone to give them a ride home.

During last summer's heat, my heart went out to the joggers. I wondered what horrible sins they had committed that made them try to extirpate their guilt by such cruel punishment. Perhaps they were trying to relieve their consciences from the guilt of telling exaggerated hunting and fishing tales.

I do what I can for joggers. I leave a hose under pressure along the front-yard curb. When I spot a staggering jogger, I turn the nozzle into a fine spray and let him stand under it until he gets his color back.

It is an act of mercy and I would do as much for any dehydrated bullfrog I found far from water. It would not matter to me that the bullfrog was guilty of folly; I would still try to help him.

Recently, I rescued a tottering jogger and brought him into my home and tucked him under a fan. After I applied ice cubes to his steaming forehead, he revived and told me he was getting in shape for the deer season. He asked if my home could become part of his regular route. He said he'd dash into the garage, come through the kitchen, pause by the fan, and then leave by the front door.

I explained that there was a better system. When he arrived home from work each afternoon, his wife should chain him to the sofa. No matter how much he screamed, she should refuse to unlock him.

It was too simple a solution and he still staggers by our house every evening. I tried to explain that you don't have to run a buck down. A bullet goes much faster than a buck. It's easier to sit under a tree, and when a buck passes you let your bullet catch up with him.

There are conflicting reports on the values of jogging and what it does to your health, assuming you survive. All I know is that I've never seen a doctor jogging. Of course, most of them get all the exercise they need by counting their money every night. It's called "pumping green."

When driving a car in the suburbs these days, one has to be careful of joggers. There's no way to predict when one might go into delirium and suddenly weave in front of you.

Joggers are usually careful when torturing themselves on main roads. They run on the grassy shoulders. I guess they want a soft place to fall when they swoon.

When you're driving and see a jogger coming toward you, he always gets the strength to raise his head and look at you. I suppose he's looking for a friend who'll drive him home.

I don't think joggers are exhibitionists like water skiers. They are sincere in their dedication. However, an oncoming jogger always looks through your windshield with such a pitiful expression that you want to play the good Samaritan.

You feel that in the name of humanity there must be something you can do to put him out of his misery. I frequently turn my car around, catch up with him, and ask if he is late for an appointment. If so, I offer him a free ride.

It's surprising how many joggers own cars. If they own cars and have to get some place, you'd think they'd drive. One jogger I tried to rescue recently told me he had three cars, all in good operating condition.

That in itself is amazing. Usually, you have to own three cars to have just one in operational order. The kids have one, another is being towed by a mechanic, and the third has been at the dealer's for a month waiting on a part.

I don't think the jogger with three cars wanted my assistance but it's hard to understand what a panting jogger wants. About all you can do is offer them succor.

I always try to be helpful to joggers. They appear to be in such agony. Whenever I pass one, I ask if he'd like a cigarette or a can of cold beer.

The offer seems to give them a lift. They nearly always raise their arms and wave a clenched fist at me, or some similar signal.

Last year, my neighbor began jogging three months before the deer season. He and I always hunt together the first three days. Old Dog Trot, as he became known, was determined to hunt far back in the woods away from all other hunters.

The night before opening, Dog Trot's wife phoned and said he could not go. I immediately walked across the street to see what had happened to my companion. He was propped up in a lounge chair sipping a health drink and suffering from advanced bunions, charley-horses, knee-jerk, Achilles' tendon, shimmies, and chronic exhaustion.

I insisted that he go deer hunting the next morning. I drove him to the woods early and manhandled him to a stand about fifty yards from the car. When I returned at noon, he was sitting comfortably with a big smile on his face. He pointed at a clearing, and I walked over and found a dead buck with antlers ready to be measured for the Boone and Crockett records.

That evening he phoned the whole town and asked them to drop by and see his big buck. He told every last one of them that he owed all of his hunting success to jogging. The next time he faints on my lawn, I'm going to let him lie there.

Putting Out the Fire

As I piled piñon logs on the campfire, I knew they would not burn evenly for cooking. The unexpected rain which had drenched the high country the night before had soaked everything, even flooding the trench around our tent and seeping into the bedrolls.

We were north of Tapicitoes on the eastern side of the Continental Divide. A few peaks were spotlighted in the San Juan Mountains, east of the Rio Brazos, but purple shadows below were covering the canyons and arroyos as if to keep them warm through the chilly night.

Rafael, my Jicarilla Apache guide and friend of many hunts, had hobbled the horses and was watching me. No matter how I changed the logs and moved around the fire, the smoke kept following me. The piñon resin would smoulder and suddenly explode, cascading smoke and sparks into the fading sky. I rubbed my eyes and moved halfway around the fire and stood, watching the smoke change and follow me.

Rafael laughed, his white teeth glistening. "The smoke likes you. It follows you everywhere."

[131]

As the smoke caught up with me again, I moved a quarter of a circle and poked at the offending logs. Rafael folded his arms across his stocky chest, leaned back on his heels, and said in his deep baritone, "Are you sure you want to do the cooking tonight?"

It was our last night in camp and I had bragged that I would show him how to tenderize deer liver from a tough old mule deer with my favorite French recipe. I had even brought along a bottle of Marsala. The frijoles were bubbling in a blackened bean pot and chili peppers were ready to be added.

An hour later, Rafael put down his aluminum plate and grunted. "You cook better than you make fires."

In all modesty, I had cooked the liver just right, with a slight hint of pink near the center and only a few ashes burned into the outside. Of course, Rafael insisted on too many chili peppers for the beans when white onions would have been better.

The night air was creeping down the steep slopes and easing along my shoulder blades. I rubbed my eyes and moved closer to the fire. I was too pleasantly full to walk over to the tent for my jacket and I stood silently absorbing more smoke.

Rafael sat on a log, his knees drawn up to his chin, staring into the fire. The smoke drifted my way and began to caress my face, sifting into my nostrils and lingering. I wondered why it always followed me and never Rafael.

I edged around to the other side of the fire, looking skyward to see a comet blazing through the clear air on its journey to eternity. I settled on a stump and waited for the smoke.

There was a crackle in the logs and a sudden flickering of orange flames which as quickly died down. The smoke began to drift around the circle of blackened logs. I stared into the few flicks of flame, the fire struggling to stay alive but at the same time burning out the energy it needed for survival.

A puff of smoke drifted into my eyes and hung there but I did not move. I was tired of trying to dodge the ashy mist. Now I knew what it really was! The Great Spirit had sent the smoke to plague me. It was like life itself, always some problem. All I wanted to do was sit by this fire forever and never go home, just stay in these mountains with my friend. But the nagging smoke was trying to keep me from enjoying these last precious moments.

It was always this way. Back in my other life in the city I could never truly relax and enjoy life because new problems kept blowing my way, always following me. I worked hard fifty weeks a year staying alive on the dreams of returning to the mountains for only two weeks.

Like the fire, I was burning myself out, and how many more bursts of flame would there be before all was consumed? Before the ashes drifted with the smoke and vanished?

Life seemed to be one endless problem after another, with the promise that when this one was solved everything would be smooth sailing. But it never worked that way. At the very instant one problem was cured, another took its place. When the house mortgage finally was paid off, the city and county doubled taxes. When the two cars were paid for, they were worn out and had to be replaced. When the kids got through high school, there was more expense for college. When the older boy graduated, he needed help to start his new office.

The things I really wanted to do were always getting shoved back. Every time I planned a weekend hunting trip, the boss asked me to go out of town or some civic club put me on a new committee or the church started another drive. Why was I always doing things I didn't really want to do? Somehow it didn't seem right to struggle fifty weeks a year to get only two when I could go hunting in the mountains. Why did I have to go home? Why couldn't I stay two more weeks?

A gust of cold air whipped new oxygen into the smouldering ends of the pine logs and the white billowing smoke changed to blue. It soared upward and left me, the air clear around my face. The problem smoke was gone! I could breathe deeply. I could see, perhaps for the first time in years.

I stood up and shouted, "Rafael, I've made a decision!"

He did not move but simply raised his eyes and stared. I thought the fire had hypnotized him.

"Rafael, you have seen how the smoke has hounded me?" As I unzipped my britches, I said, "Stand back." He jumped to his feet and moved toward the brush as I began to spray. At first there was a huge cloud of smoke from the sputtering ashes, but then it quickly disappeared and the night was clear. Everything was clear!

"Tomorrow," I shouted, "you go back to Tapicitoes for supplies. I'm going to stay for another two weeks."

"But your reservations?" Rafael exclaimed. "What about your job?"

"My attitude is exactly the same as I just demonstrated on that damned smoke!"

Coons Ain't Convenient

The trouble with hunting raccoons is that the coons are usually in some place that's hard to get to. They're always some place else, like the other side of the mountain or across the swamp. No coon is ever found on *this* side of the creek, or even *this* side of the county.

Most coon hunters use four-wheel-drive vehicles or pickup trucks. They drive as far as they can in the mountains or swamps. When they can't go any farther, they put leads on their hounds and walk them a couple of miles. Then they cut the dogs loose.

The owner of the dog that makes the most commotion wins.

The highest population of coons actually occurs around and within suburbs. The raccoon is a highly adaptable mammal and lives well on junk food thrown out of car windows. Coons are also adept at opening garbage cans, although they most enjoy turning them over.

Raccoons in the woods start rambling for food about dusk. In the suburbs, they wait until most people are in bed. *Then* they clank the garbage-can lids. Even if you use plastic cans, a prowling raccoon can make cymbals out of them.

Suburban raccoons love noise, especially just before you're about to go to sleep. They know the sizes of all the dogs in the neighborhood and which ones bark the loudest. They'll tantalize a big Labrador retriever until he's about to tear down a chain-link fence. After the Lab gets all the nearby dogs barking, the coon will amble a block away and get a new batch to yelling.

I've never seen a coon in the woods as big as some of the waddling suburban coons grown fat from turned-over garbage cans. There's a rumor that the bandits always wash their food before eating it. Well, suburban coons don't! Of course, I've seen a couple of them draining old booze bottles and beer cans. But they never wasted it by washing their hands.

There was an old bandito that liked to work our backyard at 3 A.M. Naturally, it's against the law to discharge a firearm in the suburbs. This particular coon loved our television antenna, despite the abundance of trees. He seemed to be fascinated by the bare limbs of the antenna and loved to twist and bend them in all directions.

After paying several repair bills approaching the national debt, I bought an air rifle to discourage him. The problem was that he was so fat the BBs didn't make much impression, not when the coon was swinging happily on the top of our antenna.

One morning, at exactly three o'clock, I heard the coon swinging on the antenna. I jumped out of bed and screamed, "I don't care what the gun laws are. A man has a right to protect his property and get a good night's sleep!"

While my wife pleaded with me to go back to sleep, I ran to the gun cabinet and grabbed a .22 rifle. I dashed into my den and finally found a box of cartridges. Then I rushed outside, dressed only in my undershorts.

But the wily old bandito had become suspicious with all of the doors banging. As I ran through the back yard, he was leaping off the roof to a small tree in the front yard. By the time I got through the gate, the coon was down the street.

I did what any hunter would do. I gave chase. Looking back on that night, I may have been overly agitated. The two deputy sheriffs who stopped me said later that I was waving the rifle dangerously, screaming in an unknown tongue, and running around in my underwear.

They testified that I looked rather suspicious. Further, they had seen no fleeing raccoon.

Things might have gone better for me but, when the deputies rang our front doorbell to verify my identification, my wife said she didn't know me. I can't imagine why she felt compelled to add that I looked like the flasher who had been entertaining the neighborhood.

The trouble with coon hunting with hounds is that the dogs usually tree one. The hounds put up so much racket that you have to go to them. It's the only way you can relieve their suffering. You could burn their kennel down and they wouldn't make that much racket.

Several years ago, when a raccoon hide was worth about ten bucks, I went hunting one night with some Kentucky mountain boys. The dogs were cut loose near a ridge cut and they took a beeline for the next ridge. I don't know how the dogs knew there were no coons on the ridge we were on. It looked just like the distant ridge the hounds preferred.

I was afraid they'd find a coon, and sure enough, one of the dogs struck. Naturally the coon headed for the third ridge, and the mountain boys whooped and joined the chase. I didn't want to be left in the woods by myself, so there was nothing for me to do but stumble, trip, and fall in behind them.

The boys said it was a good chase. That is, the coon was a runner and not a climber, and it took the hounds a long time to tree him. I would have thought the shorter the chase, the better.

The coon didn't go up a tree but climbed a sandstone cliff and went into a crevice. From where the coon perched, it was forty feet to the top and forty feet to the bottom. The dogs kept trying to scale the cliff, and they'd get about fifteen or twenty feet above the talus and then lose their grip and go bouncing down.

A good coon dog doesn't care how bloody he gets. In fact, there's a saying among coon hounds: "If you ain't bloody, you ain't been hunting."

One of those old Kentucky boys, who was built as lean as the hounds, ran back to where we'd started from and got a coil of rope out of a pickup truck. We anchored one end of the line around a big oak tree and he tied the other around his middle. It was pitch dark as we all grabbed the rope and lowered him.

He must not have been a good knot-tyer. The line suddenly went slack, like when a big bass throws your plug back at you, and then we heard a thud.

The dogs below thought the coon was making a run for it and they all dived in. That old Kentucky boy didn't smell like a coon, but he sure fought like one until the dogs caught on that they were wasting their time on the wrong quarry.

All of a sudden everything quieted down. As we tried to peer over the rim of the cliff into the darkness, a weak voice came from below, "Boys, come pick me up. I'm a-hurting all over!"

Three of the mountain boys volunteered to run back to the gap, then work along the base of the cliff to reach our comrade. There was no mention of giving up on the coon.

Another hunter was fighting for the chance to go over the edge. He was a lot better knot-tyer. He gave us directions as we lowered him. He finally yelled up at us, "Hold it right there! Here he is."

It turned out that the crevice wasn't any bigger than a peach basket. All of a sudden the hunter screamed, "Pull me up, boys! For gawd sakes, pull."

In all of the excitement, he hadn't taken an equalizer. The coon carried his. That big old boar coon had reached out and clamped down on his ankle. We pulled as hard as we could. The dogs were excited and yelling, the hunter was kicking with one leg at his other leg, and I guess the coon thought he was on an elevator.

Anyway, when we got the hunter to the top of the cliff, the coon jumped off and headed down the ridge. The hunter was considerably chewed up. To prevent infection, he poured some 114-proof alcohol on it that had been made the day before. Then he thought about it a second and took a big dose for internal protection.

It took an hour to go back to the gap, fetch the dogs, and then pick up the trail. The hounds chased that old boar until an hour after daylight, and finally the coon treed. One of those old Kentucky boys took out a .22 pistol and shot him.

We were six miles from the pickup truck. One of the Kentucky boys said, "There ain't nothing as satisfying as an honest night's work. That hide will bring at least $11."

The best I could figure, I lost more hide than the coon did. I heard later that the hunter who wasn't much good at tying knots got out of the hospital three weeks later. He went coon hunting that night, and the next morning he went by his home to see how his wife was doing.

A top coon dog is worth about as much as a Volkswagen, but the dog doesn't get near as good mileage. You have to feed him, whether he's running or not.

Hunters argue a lot about what's the best breed of coon dog. There are blueticks, redbones, Julys, Walkers, and mongrels. They all have one thing in common. They'll get lost on you.

Sometimes only one dog in a pack gets lost. Other nights the whole pack gets itself lost. If you don't like to look for lost dogs, you'll never make a coon hunter. Just when you think the hunt is over, that's when you start hunting—for dogs.

Anytime you've been hunting coons awhile and all your dogs are around, that's a good time to gather them up and quit. Don't worry about how many coons you've treed.

There are two main times when you can be sure at least one dog will get himself lost. When the edge of a cold front hits, and the bottom of the thermometer falls out, one or more dogs will disappear. The other time is when it starts to rain, especially one of those set-in kinds where you get to wishing you had thought about building an ark.

Old-time coon hunters say not to worry when you lose a dog. Just put your jacket down and go on home. The dog will find the jacket, lie down, and wait until you pick him up a day or two later. The most jackets I've ever lost that way in a single season is nine.

Fox hunters love to cut a big pack loose, build a fire near the top of a knoll, and sit around and listen to the dogs. Every last one of the hunters will swear his dog is leading the pack. To hear the fox hunters tell it, there must be thirty dogs running broadside.

The only way I can tell which dog is which when they're running at night is to put down just one dog. You can get by hunting raccoons with only one dog, but most hunters prefer three to six. There's more confusion that way.

Coon hunters love to build fires and stand around and brag about dogs they owned years ago, which nobody present ever saw. This gives them a lot of latitude in stressing good points. Usually what happens when you build a fire is, just as it starts roaring good, that's when the dogs tree on the other side of a swamp.

The best kind of clothes to wear for coon hunting are those you get from the Salvation Army. If you wear new hunting clothes and they last for three hunts, then you know you bought a superior brand. There are a lot of things in the woods that don't glow at night, such as sawbriars, stumpholes, rattlesnakes, and barbed wire. You may have noticed that a lot of coon hunters have tenor voices.

No matter where coon hunters are from—Arkansas, Ohio, or Alabama—they have one thing in common. They can instantly spot a tenderfoot, a city dude who's a little fleshy, unscarred, and out of shape. That's the target of the night!

What those coon hunters are going to do is to run that tenderfoot to within an inch of his life. If they're hunting in the mountains, they start by going straight up the highest one around. They'll detour five miles to be sure of running that tenderfoot through the only swamp in the county. They'll trot him through brambles, thickets, and jungles.

What they like to do is see how loud a tenderfoot can gasp. They like to peel him with bouncing limbs and, when he's down to his underwear, they want to see how tough his hide is. If there's a footlog across a creek, they're anxious to see how good a balance the tenderfoot has in the dark, especially when someone has run ahead and greased the log.

They're not actually sadistic. As far as I know, the old veterans have never left a tenderfoot in the woods to die, even if it took four of them to tote him out.

Whenever I go hunting with a new batch of coon hunters, I immediately explain to them that I'm a specialist. I'm an expert at staying at the pickup truck to guard it from attack by angry coons. To keep them happy, I always have a roaring fire when they return and plenty of hot coffee, sandwiches, and other refreshments.

Go Easy on the Pyracantha

For many years, I have zealously read publications issued by the National Wildlife Federation on how home owners can plant food and cover for suburban wildlife such as songbirds.

Now it appears that robins and other wholesome birds get drunk on pyracantha berries and various fruits planted by well-meaning bird lovers. I find myself in the unenviable position of contributing to the delinquency of robins.

The Federation reports that robins sometimes get so tipsy they bump into each other or fly into telephone wires and windows. In Nevada, hordes of migrating robins were seen staggering around after sopping up pyracantha berries. In Sweden, waxwings got so happy on fermented rowanberries, they dive-bombed cars.

Perhaps that explains the erratic flight and behavior of mourning doves, grouse, and waterfowl. It also gives me another excuse when hunting dove fields: "How can anyone be expected to hit a dove smashed on rowanberries?"

I have always wanted to do what I could for wildlife in the cities and suburbs. Realizing that many birds relish weed seeds, I let weeds take over both my back and front yards. Since weeds need little care and verbal caressing, I found that their culture gave me more free time for hunting and fishing. Things went well until the neighbors got up a delegation which accused me of fomenting community decay.

My prize bush, both from a decorative and ecological aspect, is a pyracantha. Other than occasionally backing into it with the car, I have given it little attention. Yet it expands each year and produces great clusters of red berries which birds scramble for and squirrels eat when they forget where they buried their acorns.

It was with a feeling of relief that I learned from Federation reports that animals feeding on fermented berries sometimes show behavior similar to humans coming home on New Year's morning. In other words, that weaving squirrel with the hiccups I saw recently was not because of *my* condition.

I have been trying to decide if I should cut down my pyracantha bush. After all, some humane group might sue me. I could wake up some morning and find people promenading around my yard with placards and banners protesting that I was debauching songbirds. A television newscaster might thrust a microphone at my face and ask, "How do you feel about making a four-month-old robin drunk?"

The latest Federation release states that Stanley Temple, an ornithologist from the University of Wisconsin, says that when a big bird gets drunk it is usually from some toxic substance and not alcohol. Temple speculates that this may be a particular way the plant discourages wildlife from eating its berries.

I think Temple may have his theory backwards. It may be the very reason robins eat them. Who knows what a robin is thinking? How does Temple know the birds don't like to get a little buzz on to celebrate? How does he know all those cheerful robins you hear singing haven't been at the pyracantha bushes?

Besides, just take a look at corn, wheat, and milo. With a little chemical change, these grains may provide a buzz. Add a few juniper berries, and you have a different concoction. No wonder doves and other gamebirds like to feed in harvested fields. I'll bet if you asked a hundred hunters if doves flew like they were crazy drunk, at least ninety-nine would say, "And then some."

Insects also tipple, according to the Federation. Butterfly hunters get their quarry drunk by putting out sugar-coated bananas. Nets are not needed. When the butterfly passes out, the collector simply picks it up and puts a pin through its head. One of these days the butterfly collectors are going to get it from those humane groups!

Of course, I've long suspected that butterflies imbibe. All you have to do is watch the way they fly. Also, they're intemperate about the way they mix their drinks. Have you ever noticed how they flit from one species of flower to another?

I cannot imagine a hunter putting fermented grain in a field feeder. Who wants to yelp up a drunk turkey? Or have his bird dogs attacked by a covey of brawling quail?

I've never been on an African safari, and after reading the Federation's report I'm not sure I want to. Elephants have the habit of feeding on various fermented fruits and becoming uproariously drunk. They get mischievous and step on people.

In South Africa's Transvaal, elephants eat the fruit of the marula tree. Apparently, the fruit ferments in the elephants' stomachs. Hunters don't have to track them; they can smell their breaths across several countries. If one has to be around drunken wildlife, I'll take robins every time.

Keep a Light Burning

Of all the outdoor equipment on the market today, the best buy is a convenient motel room.

I mean one that has a bed lamp with a bulb stronger than twenty-five watts and a bed with a headboard so that you can prop up and read comfortably.

I'm one of those unfortunate people who can't go to sleep without reading for a while. Even if I'm exhausted from hunting all day and immobile with aching muscles, I have to read something.

On a recent hunting trip with Gibby Cates, we were the guests of Ted Insley, a friendly fellow who built a cabin in the boondocks. Ted had often spoken warmly of his wilderness creation. It turned out to be considerably back of beyond.

The cabin was a little more rustic than I needed. There was no water or electricity. The only heat was from an antique stove that operates on wood but mostly generates smoke.

The toilet facilities were a reasonable distance in any direction from the cabin. The interior cubic footage for three hunters and two bird dogs was about the same as a cheap motel's bathroom. Needless to say, it rained every night.

Ted is proud of his cabin and surrounding land. It brings out the pioneering spirit in him. He likes to rough it. Besides, he goes to sleep instantly.

I accepted and adapted to everything but the lack of a reading light. We were there for four days, and I didn't have much choice. The first night Ted announced that he had forgotten the oil for the camp's lantern.

Gibby and Ted squirmed into their bunks and began to snore. All I had to read by was a flashlight with leaky batteries. On top of that, I discovered there was no reading material, not even a Gideon Bible.

It was the first cabin I have ever been in that didn't have a bunch of old mildewing catalogs and outdoor magazines. I couldn't even find a copy of the hunting regulations to read!

Thank goodness for the Food and Drug Administration. They now require food processors to state on labels just what's in a can. They required it for dog food for many years but only recently started requiring it for humans.

The sardine-can label didn't have much fascinating information and no staying power at all. The reading was terse and had no pace. It was different with the Vienna sausage labels. They had all sorts of fascinating information on nutrition.

I became so interested that I woke up Gibby to ask him if he knew that Viennas have 2 percent riboflavin. From the tone of his voice, it was evident that he had little interest in nutrition.

Just as I was really getting excited about the label on a can of pork and beans, the flashlight petered out. I was in total darkness and had barely started to read!

For a while I struck matches and read labels on tuna cans. Why, I wondered, did tuna have more riboflavin than Vienna sausage? I made a mental note to ask Ted about it in the morning.

After I read the label on a box of saltines, some propaganda on Idaho potatoes, and the nameplates on the dogs' collars, I ran out of matches and reading material.

I stirred up the coals in the iron range and found my shaving kit. It's surprising how much stuff is put into a can of shaving cream. It was one of the best labels I found all night.

My particular brand contains isobutane, polysorbate 60, sodium metasilicate, and about a dozen other things I'd never heard of. I knew if I kept discovering such exciting facts I'd never get to sleep.

I climbed into my sack and silently thought about light bulbs for half an hour. Then I tried counting light bulbs jumping over fences. Instead of making me sleepy, it only made me more awake.

I got up and raked the coals. There wasn't even enough light for me to read the patent numbers on the toothpaste tube.

I found some kindling, and when the flames sparkled, the cabin light increased to dim. Then I discovered that there was nothing more to read.

There was no wallpaper, so I studied the linoleum pattern to see if there was some hidden message. I quickly came to the conclusion that the designer was a square with no imagination at all. The only message I could decipher was that if you walk on linoleum in your bare feet it's cold.

Then I thought of the cards in my wallet. It was a good time to memorize my social security number in case I was ever on a quiz show. I also found a lot of old hunting licenses and these helped to keep the flame going.

But both the fire and reading material were soon exhausted. What do you do at 11 P.M. without light in the middle of nowhere? You crawl into your sack and think about riboflavin. Or wonder if all those strange blocks of parallel lines on every container really cheat you when you go through a supermarket checkout line.

Pen Pals

Wade Parmelee has been about as loyal a hunting friend as I've had the past twenty years or so. We live in different states but he keeps me informed of his hunting trips with a monthly letter of several pages. When he describes cooking deer liver and onions over a campfire, you can taste it, and every once in a while you reach up to brush cinders out of your hair.

I'm not much of a hand at writing letters, especially during fall and winter, but I always try to answer Wade. My one-page letter is a good trade to get his eight or ten pages describing his hunts. It's almost as if I'm on the hunts with him.

The strange part of our relationship is that I have never met Wade, much less hunted with him. We became pen pals through an ad he ran, looking for Chincoteague canvasback decoys made before World War I. I happened to know an old codger that had a brace, and sent Wade the name and address.

Wade was so appreciative that he sent me an old book on duck hunting on Long Island Sound. It was a collector's item of sorts, so I felt obliged to send Wade a gift. As I recall, it was a mounted set of Cherokee arrow points used for bird hunting. A few days later, I received a gracious letter from Wade with a great deal of information on the current woodcock flight.

I was not anxious to acquire a pen pal. It was hunting season and I was behind with correspondence connected with my job. Also, I was several years behind with letter-writing to relatives, old buddies, and conservation agencies. I was ready to drop the budding relationship.

But I didn't know Wade. In a few weeks I received a letter saying that he was thinking of buying a new rifle for whitetail deer hunting. He wanted my expert advice on whether to buy a .270 or a .30-06.

Well, Wade might not have known a lot about buying a rifle, but he sure understood the psychology of a hunter. No one had ever called me an expert before, so I sat down and wrote several pages on the advantages of the two calibers, and for good measure threw in the .243, .257 Roberts, and .308.

Wade eventually decided on the .270, and in future years, whenever he wrote about a deer hunt, he graciously thanked me for helping him make a decision. In fact, it was with this same rifle a dozen years later that he bagged a whitetail that scored 154 points under the Boone and Crockett system.

From the letters that came each fall and winter, Wade was evidently a good camp cook. He described new venison recipes he had originated and old ones he had modified. He always included two or three recipes for testing. Then, as a teaser for me to reply, he'd ask if I had any different ways of cooking venison. He always had a few direct questions that required an answer.

I swapped many squirrel recipes with him. There was a period when we got into some heavy philosophical discussions on the use of oregano in squirrel stew. He thought a dash of it was imperative; in my opinion, it had no place in a squirrel chef's condiment cabinet. I did finally admit that a touch of bay leaves was permissible under rare circumstances.

Wade always had fascinating bits of useless information in his letters, such as, "Did you know that as many as two percent of hen turkeys have beards?" Or, "On the average, a whitetail deer goes to the bathroom 12½ times a day." Sometimes he would bait me with questions like, "Why does a ruffed grouse have white meat on the breast and a sage grouse have dark?"

Wade's letters were so beautifully and entertainingly written that it never occurred to me that he actually revealed little about his personal life at home, including what he did for a living. I did get the idea he was well off financially, because he always had time to hunt woodchucks in spring and summer and some sort of game during autumn and winter.

From his descriptions of his friends in the North Fork Deer Club, I felt that I knew them personally, or would quickly recognize them at camp. I knew who got his shirttail whacked off, who bagged the biggest buck of the season, and which hunter fell through the ice. I knew who snored the loudest, who was the first out in the chilly dawn to cut off the alarm clock, and who always asked for a third helping of Wade's venison stew.

Wade brought them all to life in his letters, and I looked forward to receiving one each month. For twenty years or so, I felt I had a whole group of warm friends in Wade's hometown.

Quite unexpectedly I had to make a business trip near his town. I decided to surprise Wade with a visit, so I rented a car and drove over.

When I knocked on the door of a modest home that Sunday afternoon, it was answered by a housewife on the wrinkled side of middle age. I instantly noticed her direct blue eyes, square shoulders, and high chin. When I introduced myself, she maneuvered me onto the porch and closed the door behind her.

She smiled and said, "I know you're one of Wade's oldest writing friends, but he hasn't been quite honest with you. He's never been a hunter, and since his car accident twenty-one years ago he can only move his right arm and neck. I owe you an apology, but Wade needed something to look forward to. He writes to hunters all over the country and dreams of being able to go himself."

She paused, and I could see her eyes moisten. "Under the circumstances, maybe you shouldn't meet Wade. But you will keep writing, won't you?"

"You bet!" I said, "And I think I can find a couple more letter-writers." As I walked to the car, I thought, "If Wade had had the chance, I bet he'd be one helluva hunter. And that little lady herself wouldn't have been so bad, either."

Secret Baits

The ego plays a large part in fishing. It's the main reason fishing secrets are never kept for long.

If an angler discovers that a Whang-Doodle lure will produce a limit of crappie, he may keep it a secret for a few hours. But he has to tell somebody! He's like a high-school boy who finally kissed a girl without spinning a milk bottle. These days, I should say he's like a grammar school youngster. He's so overwhelmed by his accomplishment that he can't contain the vital information. A little exaggeration goes with the telling, whether he's an angler or a suitor.

When a fishing buddy calls me at midnight and in a conspiratorial tone tells me to rush over to his house, I know that I am about to become privy to a fishing discovery. When I reach his home, he takes me into the garage or basement. He's not taking any chances on a member of his family overhearing. Then he feels around the windows and under the tables to see if anyone has planted a bug.

Next he brings out the family Bible. After the oath of eternal secrecy, we seal it by sticking our fingers with needles and mingling our blood. Then he whispers the revelation.

I seldom breathe a word of it to anyone before noon the next day. Of course, I only relay it to one of my most trustworthy friends, explaining that the matter must be held in confidence because a CIA agent invented the gadget and is known to have an 007 rating and be a hit man on the side.

Sometimes it takes as much as a week for the information to get back to me from another source, like a friend who phones from Mexico City and talks in pig Latin.

During the past twenty years, I must have had at least a thousand anglers tell me in confidence that the best way to catch rainbow or brown trout is to use corn for bait. In fact, one can hardly fish a mountain stream with dry flies without some little old lady calling him out and whispering that if he really wants to catch trout he should bait up with corn.

Naturally, after twenty years, there are corn variations. One secret is to buy cheap canned corn. It's tougher and stays on the hook longer. A neighbor of mine, who will not admit that he fishes with corn, soaks his kernels in sardine oil. He accidentally told me when his family was away and he was concocting Black Russians for immediate consumption. A too generous portion of vodka freed his inhibitions.

The next day he came to my house and on bended knees begged me not to give his secret away. To stop his crying, I told him that I would confide my deepest secret. Right on the spot, I invented a story to give him solace. I told him I had discovered that trout crave vodka, and the smell of it in a stream would pull them over rocks, rills, and waterfalls.

You bought a particular brand of canned corn noted for its large kernels. Then, with a hypodermic needle, each kernel was filled with 100-proof vodka. All of the kernels were then put in a wide-lid bottle for ease of retrieving while fishing, with more vodka added for seasoning.

Three weeks later he came back from the mountains with seven of the largest rainbow trout I have ever seen in one ice chest. He told me he had improved the vodka formula by adding a secret ingredient. Then he clammed up! He absolutely refused to tell me the name of the key chemical.

At first I was indignant. But on second thought, I calmed down. He will have to tell someone! His ego demands it! It may cost me a lot of Black Russians, but I will find out. If not that way, it will come by a circuitous route through Canada, or the U.S. Fish and Wildlife Service will put out a pamphlet.

Cheese is another "secret" bait of trout anglers. It undoubtedly started with inexpensive processed cheese. Now the underground reports recommend limburger, Wisconsin gouda, Vermont cheddar, and caraway Edam spiked with port. It's no wonder so many of our streams are polluted!

Trout are known to hit doughballs, sometimes called "Sunbeam flies." Since catfish and carp search for food by scent, strong doughballs are a standard bait. A basic recipe is one cup of yellow cornmeal, one cup of flour, one teaspoon of sugar, one cup of molasses, and a quart of water. The cornmeal, flour, and sugar are made into a dough and boiled in molasses and water for three minutes.

Recently, I received a midnight call and was told to put on a trench coat, pin a rose to my lapel, and go to the bus station. As I stood by the ticket counter, a man wearing a ski mask came by and put a locker key in my hand and kept going.

I went to the locker and opened it. There was an envelope sealed with red wax. The cutout newsprint on the envelope said, "DRiVe to A CEmetAry and REad. ThEn BuRN! A FRIEND."

I followed the instructions, first driving around town for an hour to make sure I was not being followed.

Parked between two tombstones, I read by a dim car light, "For your doughballs, cut down on the molasses and add two bottles of strawberry soda and three teaspoons of orange marmalade. This mix is guaranteed to pull catfish and carp across dams!

"Use with caution. The fish may become so agitated they will jump in the boat to get at your bait bucket and swamp your boat. Also, if you spill any of the mixture, you may get your feet chewed off.

"Do not reveal this formula to anyone. I am a member of the Black Hand. You are being watched at all times."

My friend sure put a lot of unnecessary pressure on me. I've been making doughballs that way for years!

Ask a Spider

There's a saying among hunters that if you want to know a man just spend a day with him in a duck blind.

If you want to know yourself, try spending a day alone in a duck blind.

I seldom hunt alone, but I'm always glad when I do because I learn new things about myself. I can't sit in a blind all day keyed up in anticipation of the next shot. My nerves won't stand it. Besides, nature's rhythmic symphony of waves, soothing sun, and chattering winds eases my drifting mind into aimless meanderings, much like an autumn leaf floating with a changing river.

Sometimes, in a lonely marsh, my mind strays into limbo, a kind of trance. I don't seem to think of anything. I soak in the quietness and my being melts into the grass and cattails and I am a part of the whole as much as a clam burrowing in the black muck or a frog shagging bugs with his elastic tongue.

It is not necessary for me to think. That is one of the reasons I go there. For a few precious hours, I do not *have* to do anything. For this brief interval, I renounce all debts, obligations, and duties. I have no guilt feelings. These flying moments are mine!

It is deliberate escape, a time for resting the mind. There are no billboards, telephones, bosses, preachers, kith, or kin. There are no reformers, militants, newspapers, or civic leaders. There is no one exhorting me to do something constructive.

It is my time in the sun! If I wish to talk with seagulls, there is no person to laugh at me. I often talk with them, although I prefer calling white egrets. Passing crows or red-winged blackbirds are always anxious to start a conversation, too.

Golden moments come and go but I do not know how many more will come. Sometimes I watch contrails streaking across the sky, the offending aircraft so high it is not visible. The moving white vortex seems to be chasing the intruder and I raise my fist and scream, "Airplane, get out of my marsh! You don't belong here!"

As the airplane obeys my command, a coot swims up, takes a look at my decoys, and chuckles, "Phoney, phoney, phoney." I rattle the shells in my coat and the coot looks at the blind. Perhaps the curious bird has not had a surprise all day. I stick my head over the blind, and the coot and I look at each other for an instant. "Boo," I shout, and the coot frantically pounds the surface to gain airspeed for his clumsy hull.

"Bang, you're dead," I yell after the departing coot. As he lifts off, he turns slowly and I see a small spot of white lime splattering from his after end. Was the extrusion an accident or did he mean it for me, a parting symbolic shot?

There are great things to ponder and conjure with when you are alone in a duck blind. A spider finishes its web, busy since sunup preparing a net in a corner of my blind. He does not know or care that I own the blind, that he is squatting on my property. He is a brave spider; I am a thousand times larger than he. The spider stares at me impudently and I wonder if I am the intruder, if I am poaching on his territory.

A blowfly buzzes by and lands on my ankle. Does she intend to dig a hole in my skin and deposit her eggs? I ease my right hand toward her, cupped for a quick grab. Swish! She is my prisoner, totally within my power.

The spider watches intently. Does he covet this morsel for his lunch? The blowfly sought to ravish my person. It would be only just if I fed her to the hungry spider.

I am faced with a decision. But I did not come to the marsh to make decisions. The quickest way out is to release the fly. I toss her high into the gentle wind and hope that she does not come back.

I look at the cumulus clouds above and they remind me of huge cotton mounds. What fun it would be to jump on them and bounce from cloud to cloud. Or I could ski down them, starting from high on the huge anvil heads and circling around and around until I came to the wispy bottoms.

But then suppose I fell off? It wouldn't matter. I would simply spread my wings and glide slowly to the marsh, hover over the blind, then gracefully land.

A whooshing sound shatters my churning imagination and adrenalin forces me back into reality. A flight of pintails, webbed feet dangling, is erratically descending toward my decoys as their wings break their vertical fall. I ease my shotgun upward, stand, and there is a moment of confusion as the pintails try to regain airspeed. Three shots crash through the air and two ducks drop onto the rippling water with a "plop" that echoes the booming shells.

When the brace of sprig is safely in the blind, I'm again free of responsibility until another flight is lured. The caffeine in the black coffee is not needed but the steaming bitterness is as comforting as swirling a snifter of rare brandy in front of a glowing fireplace.

A few hours yet to drift, to revive the innocent imagination of a lost boyhood, to soar free! A time for wonder, to unwind and to be totally one's self. Perhaps a journey back into time, down misty trails into ancient marshes when life first crawled out of the sea. A few hours alone to refresh for the daily struggles ahead.

You may well ask why I can't restore my spirit with a simple walk along marsh dikes. Why do I have to take a shotgun? My friend, I don't know. I only know that if it were not for the gun, I wouldn't go.

The ducks, the gun, the hunt, the dog, and the other hunters. These are what lead me back to the marsh each fall. They are not what make me stay. It is a great deal to ponder. In silent hours in other blinds at future times, I will give it much thought. Perhaps I will ask a spider what he thinks.

Equipped for Quail

I grew up with the school of hunters who, when they were ready to go, stopped by the kitchen and grabbed a chunk of cornbread for lunch. They took a rusty old gun out of the corner and kicked open the back door. They whistled for a rawboned pointer or two sleeping under the steps, dreaming of biscuits and gravy.

The hunter and dogs walked to the edge of the family garden. When he stopped and loaded his shotgun, the dogs began hunting. That's where the hunt started and that's where it ended later in the day.

Nobody went quail hunting in a vehicle because he couldn't afford fifteen cents for a gallon of gas, even if he owned a vehicle. It was during the Great Depression and fifteen cents would buy five shells. Whether you were on a two-hour hunt or an all-day hunt, you walked. But those were the days of patch farming and diversified cover and feed, and there were plenty of birds.

Today a lot of hunters spend more time with their equipment than they do hunting. A hunter is not supposed to suffer, and he likes the conveniences of home right along with him in the field. I wouldn't be surprised this season to see a hunting rig in the field with a portable shower.

I'm all for it. I like my comforts as much as any hunter. I just don't want to let things get to the place where I'm spending more time repairing gear than flushing coveys and following singles.

Since many hunters are gadget-happy, and have more invested in hunting equipment than in their homes, I'd like to pass along some suggestions on the acquisition and care of quail-hunting paraphernalia.

Shotguns—Take a shotgun hunting that you can hit birds with. Most of the hunters I know always seem to leave their best gun at home. Perhaps they are trying out new guns or a gun with different dimensions or one some uncle left them.

The best and cheapest place to try out a different gun is on a skeet field. If the gun doesn't fit you, why take it? You let a quail hunter miss a few birds in a row and all you hear is fifteen things wrong with his gun. He should have known before he left that the trigger pull was off, the comb was too high, or the barrel had an S-turn on it. Why did he bring it to the field in the first place?

It doesn't make much difference whether you shoot a 12-, 16-, or 20-gauge shotgun. You're not hunting a wild turkey or Canada goose, but a little bird weighing only five to seven ounces. If you put it on them, any gauge will take care of the situation.

Shells—If you have a bad day trying to hit quail, changing shot size will not help. If you can't hit with No. 8 shot, you'll keep missing if you change to No. 9.

There's one thing for sure I've learned about shot size. You let an old boy run six or seven straight with No. 8 shot and you'll never get him to use another size.

The same principle applies to shell brand. If a hunter has a hot day with Winchester shells, that's all he will shoot from then on. You can argue with him until you're blue in the face that a Western shell is identical, that it comes out of the same loading machine as a Winchester but is simply labeled differently, but he's not going to put a Western shell in his shotgun. He'll drive fifty miles out of the way to find a store that sells Winchesters.

I've thought about this shell business for a long time. I still don't believe a shotgun has a brain large enough to tell what kind of shell is being loaded into it.

Hunting boots—The first time you wear a new pair of boots, your hunting rig will break down and you'll have to walk six miles for help. The best way to break in new boots is to loan them to a teen-ager for about three days.

No matter how good your hunting rig, you'll do more walking than you probably expect, or that you're in condition to do. If you ride a horse afield, it's a foregone conclusion that sooner or later you'll have to walk home. Buy boots that are comfortable.

If you're the kind of hunter who spends most of his ground time looking for snakes, you'll find them. If they make you nervous and interfere with your shooting, you'll be more at ease with snake-proof leather boots. If you don't have snake-proof boots, always let your hunting partner walk in front.

Hunting clothing—One of Charley's Principles is that no matter how much clothing you own you will never have the right gear along on a particular trip. If it's going to rain, it will do so when you are the farthest from your hunting vehicle.

Always buy a hunting coat and britches a size too large. You're probably not going to lose as much weight as your doctor told you to.

For Southern hunting, it is harder to find clothing in which you can stay cool on warm days than clothing in which you can stay warm on cold days. You can always add layers but there's just so much that you can take off.

The older you are, the more pockets there should be in your hunting jacket and pants. The pockets should be deep so that you can carry your pill supply, bifocals, spare parts for your hearing aid, and more shells than you could possibly use. You'll want to carry a knife, a map if you're in strange country, a compass, and matches in a waterproof container for starting a fire after you get lost.

There are many stickems in Southern quail country. Bobwhite quail instinctively scatter in palmetto, blackberry brambles, green-briar jungles, catclaw herbariums, and other barbarous things which cut and stick. The front of your hunting britches should be covered with a layer of waterproof protection, such as nylon. This keeps you from having to stay up all night after a hunt to probe for broken spears and barbs.

Hunting britches should be roomy in the bottom and knees so that you can jump a long distance in case you step on a snake. If the knees are pegged, it is difficult to cross fallen logs and squeeze between the strands of a barbed-wire fence.

If you have a large stomach, be manful and admit it. Do not try to cross over the top of barbed-wire fences or between the strands. Lie down and roll under. You may not be graceful, but it will save you a lot of tetanus shots.

Vehicles—The best kind of vehicle for quail hunting is one that will fly, has a snorkel for travel under water, and is immune to getting stuck. Unfortunately, no dealer stocks this model.

There is simply no vehicle on the market designed for quail hunting. Jeeps, Scouts, and pickup trucks, though, can be modified to meet the individual demands of hunters for their own conditions. If a hunter plans to modify a vehicle, his two best friends should be a welder and a mechanic.

The more anti-bogging equipment on a vehicle, the more likely it is that the owner will sink it. If he has a four-wheel-drive, special tires, high undercarriage, and two winches, he will think he can travel anywhere, so he will try it.

Hunters who use the family car don't get bogged down near as often. They know they are limited, so they stop at the first gate and get out and walk. They are much more likely to get home for dinner on time than many an owner of a four-wheel-drive vehicle.

There is no doubt that a modified vehicle has a lot of room for conveniences such as refreshments, spare clothing, extra dogs, gun racks, and first-aid kits. Some even have lounge chairs for the noon break. What most need is a telephone for calling a farmer with a tractor.

Lunch break—Quail don't ramble during the middle of the day. They find a nice restful spot and loaf, dust, preen, and socialize. Hunters use the same time to eat, grab a quick nap, and explain that they would have shot better if they hadn't left their favorite gun at home. The dogs get to rest before the afternoon hunt.

Until I made a couple of hunts with Duck Smith and some of his cronies at Wauchula, I had always believed that any quail hunter worthy of the name ate sardines, Vienna sausage, pork and beans, rat cheese, and saltine crackers, or some combination thereof, for lunch. In my opinion, these delicacies are much better than quail roasted over a fire, and a lot less trouble.

Duck and his buddies quickly converted me to Polish sausage cooked on a stick over an open fire the same as kids do with hot dogs. The sausage is wrapped in an oversized bun and anointed with mustard or chili sauce. If you eat two (it's impossible to stop at one) you're in ideal condition for a short, relaxing siesta.

If the weather is warm, the best bed is under a clump of live-oaks. You scoop out sand to your body configuration and it beats even a water bed. Just be sure your bed of sand does not infringe on the territory of fire ants. If they get upset with you, you'll be awake for three days and wind up with no fingernails.

Dogs—The most important thing about bird dogs is to get some that you can catch when you want to pick them up. If the dogs are hunting too close, ranging into the next county, busting coveys, or committing any number of sins, it's critical that you quickly catch them and not lose hunting time.

The longest I ever chased a bird dog was nine days, from Christmas Eve through New Year's. It was a good chance to lose the dog forever and I would not have passed up the opportunity, except for the fact that my wife loved the renegade.

It helps to have dogs that indicate by pointing where the bobwhite quail are hiding, hold until the hunters arrive, and don't chase wildly when the covey flushes. A dog should also eagerly find dead or crippled birds and fetch them to his owner.

A bird dog should have manners. That is, he shouldn't bite your hunting companions, their dogs, or you. Your dog should be honest, not try to steal the point of another, honor any dog that points first, and not argue with another dog over which will fetch a dead bird. It will save your disposition if your dog does not eat your shot birds.

If a dog hunts with courage, grace, intelligence, and style, that's icing on the cake. When you are missing a lot of birds, you can always say, "I enjoy the dog work more than the shooting."

The best strain or breed to buy for quail hunting is the one that suits you and will perform the functions outlined above.

Hunting companions—The only kind of person to hunt with is one who will not shoot you, your dog, vehicle, or other gear. If a guy thinks more of a dead quail than he does of your head, he's hardly worth cultivating as a friend.

The ideal hunting companion is a Mr. Fixit type. With all of the equipment quail hunters use these days, something is always breaking, bogging down, or hanging up. In the field, you need instant remedies. If you get snagged between two strands of barbed wire, you need someone who can free you with a minimum loss of hide and other parts.

It's best if your hunting buddy knows more about quail hunting than you and is a better shot. You'll learn more this way and he'll pull up your shooting. He should be reasonably modest when he shoots better than you. After all, you both know that for the season's average he's a much better shot. On the days when his shooting is off and you happen to do better, you can be fairly expansive. You can pink-cloud until the next trip when he clobbers you.

When you and your dogs have a horrible day afield, a good hunting buddy will let you wallow in self-pity a reasonable length of time before telling you to shut up.

Wife or girl friend—Any female whom a quail hunter gets tangled up with must be patient, tolerant, and understanding. Can a quail hunter expect to find both a good dog and a tolerant woman? Don't ask for miracles.

The Rogue

F ishing is a social sport. The participants usually fish together in clumps of two or more. It's always handy to have a buddy along to cut the hooks out of your ear.

Some kinds of fishing, such as trout fishing in streams, are solitary sports. But the trout fisherman wants company riding to and from the stream and, Lord knows, he craves someone to listen to him at night, or through the night. If no human will stick with him, a hoot owl will do. I've seen more than one trout fisherman run the camp dog off by trying to tell him the proper way to tie a Royal Coachman.

There are not many totally solitary anglers. There are a few true rogues, but fishing is not recreation to them. It is a narcotic, an escape from reality. They are emotionally immature people using practiced skills to soothe monumental egos or boost feelings of deep inferiority. They could as easily have become addicted to betting the horses or collecting pornography.

It's easy to recognize the rogue. He can watch an angler land a twenty-pound striped bass on a four-pound line and never smile or say a kind word. He looks right through the lucky fisherman. He cannot bring himself to say, "Nice going" or "That's a beauty!"

Aside from the fact that man is basically a social animal, an angler needs company in case he catches something. He wants someone to see his catch, share his joy, and admire his skill.

If you don't believe this is true, try catching an outstanding fish when you're alone sometime and never mention it to anyone the rest of your life.

A couple of years ago, I was lucky enough to spend one day fishing the streams of a wealthy trout club. The house rules permitted fishing only with dry flies, and no fish could be kept, regardless of size. I was so afraid of breaking some rule, and never being invited again, that I walked all the way back to the lodge every time I had to go to the bathroom.

The waters were frequently fertilized with fifteen-inch brown and rainbow trout. But the talk of the club was the Brown Monster, which had survived every club member's tricks for years. He lived in the Busted Line Hole.

For the afternoon fishing, I drew that stretch of stream. There was a light hatch of mayflies, and I cast an imitation onto the surface of the Busted Line Hole. While I was fiddling with my line, a hulk of brown specks slowly rolled and consumed my fly. I instantly knew it was the uncatchable monster, but my main thought was that I was going to lose another fly. I never dreamed of landing such a trout.

To hasten a long story, the fish was either dying of old age, hung over, or had a death wish. He swam toward my waders in the shallows, and I grabbed him by the tail. Whether the trout weighed ten pounds or fifteen, I don't know. Most of my experience has been with trout weighing less than a pound. Considerably less.

My first impulse was to kill the fish, sneak it into camp, and smuggle it out in my suitcase. But I hoped to be invited back and I was afraid of being caught. As I continued to hold the fish in the water, he slowly quit struggling. Then, it suddenly dawned on me that there was no one to show the fish to!

I squatted in the water with the biggest trout I had ever caught or seen outside of a hatchery, and there was not so much as a kingfisher to show him to. There was not even any way I could take a picture. Who would ever believe I caught the Brown Monster?

At that moment of desperation, I looked up. There on the bank stood a fisherman I had seen at the lodge. I yelled and raised the trout from the water. Although the angler was looking at me, the expression on his face did not change.

As he walked toward me, I noticed that he had a camera strapped around his neck. He waded to within five feet, and I made a mighty tug and lifted the trout from the water. He did not see it.

He said, "Are you sure you drew the Busted Line Hole for the evening's fishing?"

"Positive," I choked, "My hands are kind of full, but if you'll feel in my shirt pocket, you'll find the slip."

As I bent over to keep the trout in the water, he reached across, prowled through my shirt, and drew out the slip. "Odd," he said. Then, he began wading toward the bank.

"Sir," I yelled, as I raised the trout again, "would you please take my picture with this fish so that I can release it?"

Without looking back, he replied, "No."

As he disappeared upstream, I was sadly aware that I had encountered a rogue, one of the true solitaries.

I worked my way toward a big rock, still holding the trout under water. I sat down and prayed for another fisherman to come by so that I could show my fish. When it grew pitch dark and no one had wandered by, I released the fish and headed for the lodge. The trout probably would not live, but I had abided by the club rules.

During the cocktail hour I was introduced to the rogue, freshly shaven and tweedy. He said, "Your fly didn't match the hatch this afternoon."

Still on my best behavior, I smiled and said, "If you'd like to make a public statement about any large trout you saw me with, I'm sure the members would be glad to hear it." He turned, ambled to a corner, and stared at a painting.

Throughout dinner, there was much hilarity as anglers told of their catches and losses and asked friends how they had done. The rogue did not volunteer a word. I did not mention catching the Brown Monster. Who would believe me? It was as if catching the largest trout of my life had never happened.

I've thought about that afternoon a great deal the past two years. If I had done what I should have, I think any jury in the world would have let me off with a verdict of justifiable homicide.

Pouring Doubles

$\mathbf{S}$erving time in any branch of military service teaches one never to volunteer for anything. Civilians who live long enough learn it on their own. If one belongs to a sportsmen's club, he quickly gets the message.

Being chairman of a sportsmen's committee is like trying to pour water uphill. All of your work is going to run back down on you. It's not that it's difficult to get hunters to agree on anything—it's impossible.

Ten years ago, two West Virginia gentlemen—Bob Kelly and Charlie Hamilton—trapped me into being chairman of the Doubles Committee of the Woodcock Boscage Benevolent Society. The committee's duty was to define exactly what a double is in wing shooting.

When I say I was trapped, I mean it quite literally. Following a night of banjo picking and clog dancing in a clapboard hotel of Civil War vintage in Davis, West Virginia, I found myself locked in an abandoned coal shaft with an iron-grilled entrance. After two days on bread and water, while my companions were hunting woodcock in the Canaan Valley, I reached a compromise with Bob and Charlie. I "volunteered" to serve as chairman of the Doubles Committee if they would also be on the committee.

At meetings of the Migratory and Technical committees, it was decided that our work would be so valuable that it should encompass all wing shooting. It would be the definitive study. The final report would be circulated worldwide and would once and for all standardize the definition of a wing-shooting double.

After nine years of correspondence with Kelly and Hamilton, I submitted the committee's report to the full membership of the WBBS. First, I announced that killing two birds with one shot is not a double. It is blind luck. This decision was greeted with considerable foot-scraping and booing, immediately identifying those who had recently lucked out.

Copies of the committee's definition of a double were distributed to the members. It read: "A double is when a shotgunner knocks down one bird with one shot and with no perceptible stop in movement quickly kills another bird on the wing with a second shot."

The committee's definition was instantly rejected by a chorus of owl hoots, panther screams, and dying-rabbit calls. Because a double has great prestige and is a year-round source of conversation, the members wanted the definition relaxed.

A South Carolina member proposed a special category for bobwhite quail. On a covey rise, for instance, if three shots are fired, with continuous movement and no balking by the hunter, it should be called a double if any two quail drop.

Where a hunter killed a quail on the first shot, missed the second, but connected on the third, it should be known as a "stutter double."

A Minnesota duck hunter proposed a category to be called a "mercy double." If on the first shot he hit a duck and it wavered but did not plummet, it would be his duty to fire a second shell to dispatch the bird. If on his third shot he downed a duck, and there was no pause in his action, then he should be credited with a "mercy double."

A Texan wanted a category for a "gun-jam double." If he killed a bird with the first shot but could not fire a second because the gun jammed, he should be allowed special dispensation. After repairing the gun, if he bagged a bird on the first shot, it should be ruled a "gun-jam double."

A New York woodcock hunter wanted the definition broadened to allow for the low daily limit. When he shot his last bird of the daily bag and there was another in the air, he could not shoot. If he could have legally fired, he might have gotten a double. He proposed calling this a "virtual double."

A Connecticut grouse hunter said that if this was accepted, he proposed a "seasonal double." If on his last shot of one season he killed a grouse and on his first shot of the next season he downed one, then he should be credited with a "seasonal double."

An old codger from Michigan wanted this modified. If he was ill enough to miss a hunting season, practically dead, but on the last shot of the preceding season he had killed a bird and on the first shot of any post-recovery season he should down a bird, then it would be called a "hiatus double."

An unknown deer hunter wanted to know the classification of his shooting if he shot one buck, then the bullet passed all the way through and killed another buck standing behind. The sergeant at arms immediately ejected him, a rifleman having no business in an assembly of wing shooters.

One hunter proposed that a referee, wearing white knickers and a black-and-white striped shirt, should accompany all woodcock hunters shooting for record. The referee would be the final judge in all questions of doubles or triples.

The society's attorney remarked that referees cannot see any better than hunters. They should be required to carry a portable television camera for instant replay before making a decision.

To end the debate, I made a motion that all pump and semi-automatic shotguns with a capacity of more than two shells be outlawed. The membership shouted for a vote. The result—I was kicked off the Doubles Committee—unanimously.

When I returned to my motel room, I discovered a definition of a double with which no one can argue. It's two ounces, or twice the portion the pourer would dispense if he were building a single.

The Long Flight

Canada geese make a joyful noise. At least their cahonking sounds that way to me.

They're glad to arrive in autumn with their goslings and happy to leave in the spring for their remote breeding grounds. When they begin cranking up for a feeding flight, they let the world know about it. On the return to their resident lake, they're glad to get back.

It doesn't matter much what they're doing—feeding, loafing, or squabbling—they seem to be having a good time. I like their attitude.

I never see or hear wild geese without thinking of my old hunting friend, Ed. I never knew his age for sure but he began shooting geese when the daily limit was thirty-two, back when it was legal to use live decoys.

Ed used to tell grand stories of the old days. He lived in central North Carolina but each fall he went to Currituck Sound or Lake Mattamuskeet to go fowling. When the limit of thirty-two was drastically reduced to sixteen, Ed hung up his 32-inch double and swore he was through hunting.

He ranted and raved about it all spring and summer but when the cold nights came Ed took his double off the rack and headed for Mattamuskeet. Sixteen geese a day were hardly worth fooling with but he couldn't stay away from their music.

When the limit was dropped to eight, Ed spent the off-season writing congressmen and telling them why he had stopped hunting. Nobody but an idiot would make a three-week trip to the coast to hunt fowl with a meager limit of eight.

But when the leaves started dropping that fall, Ed got itchy. He decided that even a small number of geese was better than no geese at all. The same thing happened when the daily limit was lowered to four.

I first met Ed when the limit had dropped to three. He had retired and built a cottage right on the shore of Lake Mattamuskeet. I soon realized he was lonely. His wife had died years before and his children were scattered. I guess he figured all he had left were the Canada geese.

Ed arrived the same date each September, about twenty-four hours before the first flights were due in. Their migrations run on schedule. Ed was there to listen to the first family groups settling in and then the massive flights of cahonking geese announcing their arrival.

When I first knew Ed, about 125,000 Canadas wintered on Mattamuskeet, so many the Feds hoped they'd scatter. Later on, when the geese began stopping in Maryland, the limit dropped to two at Mattamuskeet and finally down to one. Ed even set his own limit. He'd shoot one goose for Thanksgiving and another for Christmas.

But if you visited at Ed's cottage, he rousted you out of bed two hours before sunrise to sit in his blind in a leased cornfield. If it had been a bright night, you'd have scattered flocks returning to the lake. Along about first light, a few lead geese would begin tuning up on the lake, quickly joined by others as scouts made test flights over the corn and soybean fields.

When thousands of geese chimed in, the rumble became a steady hum and roar, individual cahonking blended into a solid clamor. You knew the geese would soon be flying, breaking into small flocks to fan out for miles. If you were lucky, or did a good job of calling, some of the flocks would try to land in your decoys.

Ed always carried his old double to the blinds, but in later years no shells. He seemed content to sit and listen. Sometimes he'd ask me to shoot a goose for his Lab to retrieve. I suspected that Ed was losing his sight.

One morning as we shivered in the blasts of a nor'easter, Ed turned his gaunt face toward me and said, "When I die I'm going to become a wild goose."

I tried to laugh it off by saying, "Ed, you're half goose now. You understand goose talk better than most geese."

"I mean it," he said. "When the geese go back to James Bay next March I'm going with them."

When I left the cottage in December, Ed pleaded with me to come back in late March, even baiting me with the promise of good bass fishing. I told him I'd come by for a few days.

When I arrived in March, the days were getting longer and the geese were restless. Ed, wearing his old wool sweater, was resting in a lounge chair in his yard listening to the geese chatter on the lake. "They'll try to leave me tomorrow," he said.

The sun was bright and warm the next morning as I waded the shallows casting a topwater plug. About mid-morning the geese suddenly became excited.

Small flocks took off and flew up and down the lake calling to those on the water. Then more and more geese took to the air and began forming into loose Vs. The flocks of a dozen became a hundred and these joined into larger groups, every goose cahonking joyfully. Soon nearly every goose was in the air trying to join some formation.

The calls, indeed the whole clamor, became a high-pitched pleading, an excited appeal to join up for a great adventure. As the geese gained altitude, the great formations smoothed out, circled the lake twice, and then took a heading just east of north and slowly vanished, their joyful sounds slowly fading.

When I returned to the cottage, Ed was stretched out in his lounge chair, smiling peacefully. His eyes were closed and I knew that he had left on his long journey.

The Joy of Whooping

For the truth of the matter is that man is not as much of a thinking animal as he likes to believe.

In the trivia of making more money than he needs to live, so he can buy another gadget that will break down, he neglects his senses. Or they become so abused by the artificial hammering of living in habitat far beyond carrying capacity that they become buried remnants lying dormant.

These ancient senses, which are a part of our personality and very being, crave exercise and expression. When we free ourselves from the straitjacket of city living, our senses burst loose and gurgle as happily as a mountain stream bounding from a glacier to a green valley.

Although we don't think much about it when we go hunting, one of the reasons we enjoy it so much is that we let our senses unravel and flow. We let go. We relax and become ourselves.

Each New Year's, I like to reflect on the things I have seen and heard and smelled in the past year of hunting. I know it is too easy to

[175]

forget, or to submerge these precious memories too deep in the bog of daily living. I need to recall them, to nourish and keep them fresh, always handy to restore my being and remind me of what I am.

If one sits quietly in a dim room with the warmth of an oak fire soothing the air waves, the old hunting smells will return again. Some of the smells may not be pleasant but they will make you alive. There is the rank musk of an angry polecat that saturated a careless bird dog, an irritating odor that lingered for days after the hunt.

There is the coarse smell of a black bear, his hair wet from breaking through laurel bushes. If it is early autumn and the blueberries are lush, there is the sharp smell of gorging and running bowels. There is instant communication, a reminder that you do not want to crawl on your hands and knees in the laurel hell and that you may suddenly find yourself disputing a broken path with a gluttonous bear.

Most of the wafting odors are more subtle. The dank moisture of green moss clinging to a wet rock or the woody smell of a rotting log broken open for kindling. The walnut leaves smell one color when damp and another when dry.

At home you may never notice the welcome smell of percolating coffee, but at camp it seeps into your fiber with a warm sense of anticipation and joy. You will never forget the aroma of bacon fat sizzling in an iron skillet as your stomach acids bubble for relief. And what of the hot biscuits, clumsy clods of browning dough reeking with ravenous promise?

You savor each bite at a campfire. In the city, you rush breakfast to get to work and five minutes later you do not remember what you had. It would not matter if you did. For lunch, it's something you do with your hands while you are conducting business, and in the evening eating is a routine while you listen to a news broadcast of gloom which you did not need to know.

At home, getting out of bed is a struggle, something you must do that you do not want to do to go some place you'd rather not be. But at a hunting camp, dawn is an adventure. There is excitement and anticipation and the glow of great things about to happen. We could close our eyes and feel the sun coming up, the subtle changes of temperature creeping along our necks and shoulder blades. A morning breeze ruffling dry leaves and birds chattering hello tell us that everything is starting all over.

We must remember these things. We must store them and save them. We do not need to think about them, talk about them, or analyze them. All we need to do is let our senses absorb them and saturate our being.

Many years ago in southeast Ohio, I let my ears soak in the joyful sounds of another human being on a cold New Year's afternoon. I was poking along a hardwood knoll with a hammer .22 hoping to get a shot at a rambling squirrel. In the distant stillness, I heard someone hollering. Thinking someone might be in trouble, I walked in the direction of the sounds.

The hunter, or whoever he was, kept shattering the air with joyful yells. Whatever his problem, he was in no danger. My curiosity raised, I moved silently toward him. When I reached the top of one of the rolling hills, I could hear him clearly from the next hill across a small valley. He was no more than two hundred yards away, and finally I saw him sitting on a large rock, a gun cradled in his lap. He cupped his hands, reared back, and gave a long yell.

Forgetting about squirrels, I settled comfortably against a log and spied on him. Every minute or two, he would rear back and yell or whoop. Sometimes it would be a series of short yells and the next a long, drawn out holler. I must have watched him for an hour before I realized there was no purpose in his yelling except for the pure animal joy of yelling.

The more I listened to him, the more I wanted to yell. Why did I have to have a purpose? If he was yelling for the sheer pleasure of being alive, so could I. I took a deep breath and let go a high yell. For an instant, he was startled. He peered my way, but I could not tell if he saw me. If he did, he did not bother to wave. He threw back his head and let go with a corker, one that lasted about a minute.

I answered back with my best war whoop. For the next two hours, we yelled and whooped at each other across that narrow valley. He came no closer and I stayed on my log. When the afternoon shadows grew long and black, I stood up and waved. He rose up from his rock, put his gun down, and waved. Then he heaved his chest and let go a resounding yell of release and joy. We turned our separate ways and went home.

I often think of my unknown friend. It was the most honest communication I have ever had with another human being.

The Best Way to Hunt Grouse

Do you get more shots at ruffed grouse when hunting with dogs or without them?

Next time the conversation lags at any place where sportsmen are, such as a banquet when you're seated next to strangers, toss this question up and in a few minutes you'll have several people all talking at the same time. The one who shouts the loudest is the one who's shot the least number of grouse.

It's a catchy question, and the answer depends on whom you ask. I have a strange plug in my tackle box with which I once caught a lunker bass. I have carried the plug several thousand miles and cast it even farther but it has never produced another fish. Yet, if someone asks about the plug, I reply, "It's a great plug! I once caught an eight-pound bass with it."

Hunters tend to remember only their most successful days, and it's a good thing! If we remembered only the bad days, we'd probably give up grouse hunting to watch nuthatches take sunflower seeds from backyard bird feeders.

If a hunter has a good day behind a dog, then that's the only way to hunt. If another gunner, slowly walking an old logging road, gets a limit without dogs, you couldn't give him the best setter in Pennsylvania.

I've conducted basic field research on both sides of the question. When I first began many years ago, I lived in the southern Appalachians, and grouse hunting was more of an endurance contest on the steep, rocky mountainsides than anything else. To keep from rolling down the mountain when a bird flushed, you held onto a tree with one hand and fired your shotgun with the other. One of the most pleasant surprises of my life was to discover that you could find grouse in gently rolling country in Wisconsin, Michigan, and parts of New England. It was easier shooting because you weren't puffing so hard that you knocked the stock away from your cheek.

In any serious discussion of the best way to hunt, one must start with the dogs. First of all, it is not easy to be a grouse dog, no matter what your lineage or schooling. The ruffed grouse is not a cooperative or consistent bird. An excellent pointing dog may wind a grouse at ten yards and lock up on a staunch point. The grouse will do one of three things, or possibly a combination of them.

Once in a while the bird will hold until the hunters arrive. The grouse may tire of the game, stick its head up, and look around, and then slink away. Or it may not want to play the waiting game at all and immediately flush, although the dog has committed no errors.

A great many innocent dogs have been tanned for the latter. The dog did not sin; the bird flushed on its own, but the hunters did not get a shot. Dogs inclined toward complexes never make good grouse dogs.

In some parts of our northern backwoods and parts of Canada, where the grouse seldom sees humans and receives no gunning pressure, it is called a "fool hen." It is often easy to walk up close enough to kill one with a rock, and you may be allowed several throws. But where the grouse has been hunted for years, it's a wild, unpredictable bird, especially during the gunning season. It is not generally realized that the grouse themselves refer to humans with guns as "fool hunters."

One must go through a lot of dogs to find one capable of handling ruffed grouse some of the time. We will not get into the economics of owning and training bird dogs. It's too depressing.

Even when a grouse decides to hold for a dog, it's probably not for long. If you use a pointing breed—setter, pointer, Brittany, or German shorthair—the dog must be a close worker, quartering through the cover no more than twenty to forty yards ahead of the hunters. If the dog happens to point, the hunters should get to him as quickly as they safely can. The grouse may flush at any instant, and the closer the hunters, the better their chances of getting off a round or two.

If you prefer a dog that flushes, such as a Labrador retriever or a springer spaniel, the dog should quarter in front of the hunters at no more than twenty yards. Even ten yards is not too close if the hunters walk slowly and give the dog a chance to work out the cover. When a Lab or a springer gets birdy, his tail wag accelerates, his hips go into a hula, and he becomes excited. The gunners need to catch up with the dog immediately because he's going to flush the grouse—assuming it's still there.

One of my favorite hunting companions is Jarvis Boone, a wood-carver from Sugar Loaf, New York. When I first started hunting with him, he was a target for anyone who wanted to donate a pointer not inclined to hunt the same county as its owner.

His liver-and-white pointer was aptly named Ranger. Jarvis had access to many grouse coverts, and there may have been times when Ranger pointed a bird. We never knew because Ranger liked to keep two mountain ranges ahead of us.

When Jarvis put the dog down in the morning, Ranger immediately became "lost" several miles away. We spent the day looking for him. On the off-chance that we might find Ranger in a covert, we combed good grouse habitat.

In the course of our search, we usually walked up several grouse and sometimes woodcock. By the end of the day, we would have a respectable bag, and when we returned to the car at dark Ranger would be there, anxious to inspect our game bags.

Jarvis, not exactly a shy person, would drive by several hunting buddies' homes to show them our birds. If we had taken more grouse than woodcock, Ranger was a grouse dog. If we had kicked up more woodcock, Ranger was a woodcock dog. Strangely enough, Jarvis built up quite a reputation as a dog trainer, and Ranger became known far and wide as a great grouse and woodcock pointer. Some hunters even got to bringing their bitches to pay courtship to Ranger.

I can't say I was unhappy when Ranger passed on and went to that great race course in the sky. In fact, I was glad when Jarvis then acquired a Labrador retriever. He did a magnificent job of training Loudspeaker to quarter every inch of cover in front of the hunters, never more than fifteen yards away.

We shot a lot of grouse over Loudspeaker—always more than we took home. It wasn't that the Lab didn't mark dead birds and find them. The dog had a craving for raw grouse and always ate the first two. If it had not been for that peculiar distraction, I would have rated Loudspeaker as an outstanding grouse dog.

One advantage of hunting with capable dogs is that they can cover more territory than a pair of hunters. When they begin to make game, or go on point, it's an indication that a bird is just ahead. It gives you a chance to prepare for a shot. You can quickly plan your approach to the dog, and possibly the grouse will not flush with a massive tree between you and him.

If you hunt dogless, there's no warning that a grouse is taking to wing. The most likely time for a grouse to flush is when you're tangled in a grapevine, over your head in laurel, or down on your knees trying to get through a briar thicket.

When a dog, whether a pointer or flusher, first makes game, it's a good idea to immediately stop him by yelling, "Woah!" This gives the hunters a chance to catch up. Then the dog is signaled forward with the hunters right behind him, so that no matter when the grouse goes up they're in shooting range. If you're hunting a pointing breed and it locks up, that's a bonus. His nose indicates where the bird is sitting, or used to be sitting.

One problem with most grouse dogs my friends own is their fluctuating hearing. If the dog is within grabbing distance, he hears you quite clearly. On the other hand, if the same dog is at forty yards and you yell "Whoa!" he does not hear you at all. I have seen and heard my friends yell "Whoa!" repeatedly, with increasing volume and frenzy, not to mention a mixture of highly descriptive words, as the dog went ahead and bumped the grouse. Obviously the dog did not hear his master.

I have a red-and-white setter afflicted with this same fluctuating hearing problem. I have tested his hearing many times. He sleeps at the foot of my bed, and it is eighteen paces through a hall and two rooms to his food pan in the pantry. Many a time I have gone into the kitchen at midnight without the dog's awakening. But if I take one meat scrap and drop it into his plastic platter with a gentle *plop,* Willie instantly appears. I am confident that his short-range hearing is excellent, but the next day afield he does not hear me yelling at forty yards or farther. One dog trainer suggested that I yell "Woe!" at Willie rather than "Whoa!" but it didn't improve his hearing.

I finally found one location where a wild-running grouse dog was an asset. In a rugged section of the Smoky Mountains in western North Carolina, there is a long stretch of railroad where the sides are steep mountains, too steep for a man toting a gun. But the foxgrapes are thick, and grouse sometimes rappel from the summits to feed.

A free-spirited dog craving exercise is sent up one of the inclines. As he hunts above the tracks, I poke along the rails. When he flushes a grouse, I may get a shot as the bird sails out across the railroad cut toward the other side. It is a productive way to hunt at times, although one has to watch out for rock slides. Also, I prefer to use somebody else's dog.

Another advantage of hunting with dogs, even though they may be bumping birds out of range, is that at least you see some grouse. This keeps you pepped up. You at least know there are birds present and that you have wisely chosen a correct area for the day.

When dogs flush a grouse, it usually flies a considerable distance, especially if the bird is encouraged by several shotgun blasts. On the other hand, if two hunters are combing a woods without dogs, a bird at some distance may simply fly up into the nearest tree, usually an evergreen. Dogless hunters are constantly watching for this because they have only themselves to depend on, whereas hunters with dogs are not as attentive and are inclined to be overly focused on the dog or yelling at him.

With dogs or without, when you mark a tree in which a grouse has just perched, this is the time for you to be polite to your companion. That is, you offer him the shot and you volunteer to go under the tree and shake it, or throw spruce cones to chase the bird out.

In fact, I *insist* that my buddy take the shot. It's the toughest grouse shot you can get! Although the bird's departure route cannot be predicted, the chances are that when it comes out it will fly downward and the gunner will shoot over it.

In a tree situation, I always tell the gunner to choose a spot where he will be clear to shoot. Then I walk under the tree and make a great show of propping my shotgun safely against a log. It is abundantly clear to the other hunter that when I flush the grouse, my duties are over. It is his sole responsibility to bag the bird.

It's a no-lose situation. If he happens to kill the grouse, I will congratulate him, and he will consider me an unselfish fellow. But the odds are that he will miss. The grouse may tower out of the tree, sail downward, or fly in such a direction that the gunner must fire through a maze of conifer needles and limbs.

When he misses, I have my options. If he is way ahead of me in shooting, I can roll on the ground with laughter. If by chance I am ahead of him, I can be noble and offer condolences. I can also bank the deposit for withdrawal a year or two later if he becomes boastful, restoring him to a reasonable state of humility for his own welfare.

With or without dogs, two hunters make the ideal party. It is difficult to keep track of more in thick cover, and one must feel free to take an unexpected shot. When hunting without dogs, the best way is to frequently change directions and every forty or fifty yards pause for a half-minute or so. This keeps the grouse guessing. It puts the pressure on them, and they're more likely to fly.

Grouse spend a lot of time in trees and are not always on the ground where a dog might pick up scent. Hunters with dogs usually walk at a steady pace, unless they're running after a dog they've been trying to catch. I think grouse perched in trees tend to let these parties pass. But dogless hunters who pause quietly and take zig-zag courses may make the birds jittery enough to fly.

An excellent way to hunt grouse without dogs is for one hunter to walk fifty yards or so ahead of the other, with coordinated pauses and course changes. A nearby grouse often lets the lead hunter pass and then flushes. The trailing hunter may get a shot.

This system cannot be used with a dog. I would never try it with one of my own dogs. I don't want some hunter fifty yards behind shooting a grouse my dog failed to find. And I would never agree to be the trailing hunter. If my dog ever locks up on a grouse, I want to be up there close to him so I can shout "Hallelujah!"

The Best Part of a
Hunting Trip

What's the most pleasant part of a hunting trip? It's certainly not pulling the trigger on a deer or elk. That only takes a second or a fraction of a second, although it may have taken a week or more to reach that moment.

There is a great deal of satisfaction in shooting a double on incoming Canada geese or ringnecked pheasants straining for distance. But there again it only takes a second or so. Besides, if I get a double, my immediate emotional reaction is not a pleasant feeling but one of surprise and disbelief. My next response is to make sure my companion saw the miracle.

Then there is the charade of acting modest about my achievement. It is a false modesty deliberately dramatized to imply that I am so used to making doubles that another one is of no consequence. There is small pleasure in it, simply a gesture to groom my ego.

To me, the most pleasant part of a hunting trip is a motel room. I hasten to add that I do not always stay in motels. I have had my share of raunchy shacks, pup tents, and bare ground. Campfires are as soothing as old brandy. Everyone should have the experience of arriving back at camp after dark and trying to start a fire with wet leaves and twigs.

My memory bank is filled with vivid pictures of camps, and I would not trade a single one. But motels have hot running water!

Some of my most pleasant memories are of Homer, now passed away. He and I used to pursue coveys of California quail in the San Joaquin Valley, which in a really wet year gets ten inches of rain. After a day of hunting, you weighed several pounds more from the deposits of black dust, and that's after losing a few pints of blood from punctures by mesquite needles.

Homer never considered staying any place except a motel, and I was not foolish enough to change his custom. Our main decision was whether to eat dinner before we went to the motel or go to the motel first, clean up, and then go to our favorite Basque restaurant in Bakersfield.

It was never an easy decision. If we went to J.B.'s first, we had a sanitation problem. After a day of stomping Kern County alkali, we looked like two coal miners who had been trapped underground for a week. I suffered from the horrible fear that if we were in an accident, such as colliding with too many Basque *chakuas* spouting red wine, and had to be undressed, someone might think I had been wearing the same underwear for a year.

On the other hand, if we went to our room to clean up, it was hard to get moving again, even with the enticement of J.B.'s platters of pickled tongue, lamb fries, and potatoes cooked in beef tallow. But no matter which we did first, the most pleasant part was finally to be propped up in bed, clean and stuffed, with the knowledge that we did not have to move for the next ten hours.

We didn't talk much. Homer always had a book to read, and I had a detective novel I'd been working on for several hunting seasons. No one ever thought of disturbing the tranquility by turning on the television set.

Although we never discussed it, the basic idea was to stay awake a couple of hours and luxuriate. It was a time to let the leg muscles relax, scratch fly bites, and think of the glories of the day. As far as I could tell, Homer never read more than a page in his book. I simply stared at the ceiling, melting into comfort and stretching my toes, free at last from my hot boots.

Once in a while Homer would heave a great sigh, a signal of utter contentment. Occasionally I would grunt, move the two pillows to the exact right spot under my head, and wonder if a happy pig in a mudhole ever felt better.

Homer's setter always conked out at the foot of his bed. Mine passed out as if dead, except for an occasional leg twitch. Sometimes during the night the dogs would wake up and eat. They were always too tired for food when we came in.

It is amazing how quickly the mistakes of the day were forgotten. Without raising his head, Homer would say, "That was a nice shot you made through the saltbush." I did not think it necessary to remind him of the single I stepped on and missed three times.

Perhaps fifteen minutes would pass, and then I'd tell Homer how well his Sioux had quartered and pointed. He'd smile fondly and grunt. I'd heave a sigh.

If there was any world outside that motel room and the memory of the day's hunt, we did not let it intrude on us. Homer would speculate on how many mesquite needles had penetrated his hide. I would wonder how many quarts of dust I had inhaled.

Although our bones were contentedly aching with exhaustion, we did not want to sleep yet for a while. It was too pleasant just to idle and bask in luxury.

Of course, we had our serious moments as well as our reveries. Homer had a technical problem which we frequently discussed.

When a single or several valley quail ran under a thick mesquite clump, it was difficult to flush them. Some clumps were so dense with thorns the dogs could not get inside. Homer would get on one side of the clump and I would take the other. We'd try to find a stick to toss to flush the quail.

The trouble was that there were few sticks lying around. The handiest and most numerous objects for chunking were cow piles. If you chose one of just the right consistency, it would sail for good range, shatter into small fragments on hitting the tops of the mesquite branches, and bombard the quail into taking flight.

Homer always planned to write a monolog on "The Best Way to Select the Correct Cow Pile for Efficient Ballistics When Flushing California Quail." To the eternal loss of the shooting fraternity, he never reached a conclusion. He always drifted off to sleep first, and I had to get up and turn out the lights.

Generation Gap

As the stepfather of three children, I've given up a lot of hunting and fishing time to make sure they were properly reared. I don't mean just taking the boy and two girls on outdoor trips but really counseling them on their futures.

I haven't had much luck with my guidance. There's a generation gap all right! I've done everything possible to encourage them to marry into families that own a lot of land. They've had complete freedom of choice. They could either marry into a family with a great amount of hunting land or one with several farm ponds or lakes, well stocked.

Of course, they could make their old dad happy and marry into a family that had both! That's really planning for the future.

All three youngsters are now in their twenties. They're not doing much to prepare for my old age. If their current romantic interests are any indication, all three could get married and not increase my land access by as much as an acre and no fish ponds at all.

Whenever our older girl comes home, I always try to escort her to rural square dances or barbecues where she'll have a chance to meet young men her age, with property. Nothing ever clicks. Recently, I took her to a barn-raising and introduced her to T. Robert Huntingdon, whose family owns some of the best bass ponds in the state.

When I dragged T. Robert over to meet her, I said, "I'd like you to meet T. Robert Huntingdon, who owns many bass ponds." My daughter took one look at him, shrugged her shoulders, and asked, "What do you do besides fish?"

Well, that was the wrong thing to ask. Everybody knows T. Robert doesn't need to work, not with all the money in his family. T. Robert figures he's working if he ties a plug on his own line.

When I caught up with my daughter, she was furious and said, "He's the most repulsive man I ever saw."

She had a case, I suppose. T. Robert is not exactly a thing of beauty, not with that pointy head and those beady eyes.

I tried to explain to my daughter that as one gets older physical looks don't mean so much. Things tend to neutralize. A ten-acre bass lake makes one forget all about warts and pimples.

I've about given up on her. She rents a suburban apartment and goes steady with a young man who comes from a long line of city dwellers. Between the two of them, the only land they own is one flower box that sits in a window. I've seen it, and it doesn't even have rich dirt!

Our boy and I have always had a good rapport. He really listens and many a time I've told him, "You see these old gray hairs? Well, that's wisdom sticking out. Sooner or later you'll get married and it might as well be into a land-owning family."

He's a fine boy and likes to bring his dates by home for his mother and me to meet. For a while he showed some promise. One night he came by with Sarah Dithers, whose family owns a large dairy farm.

When they left, I said to my wife, "I hope nothing comes of it."

My wife looked surprised. "It's only their first date, but Sarah is certainly a fine girl."

"Yeah," I replied, "but there's not a fishing pond on her place and the cows don't leave enough cover to hide a rabbit."

Shortly afterwards, our son started going steady with the daughter of a professor in the local college. That was five years ago and they're still going steady. She's a lovely girl in every way, but she has one handicap.

The only land her family owns is a one-acre homesite in town. There's some good cover on it but it's in the wrong place. As far as I've been able to find out, her old man doesn't have a single contact with pond owners, and he doesn't even hunt.

Our younger daughter doesn't hold out much hope. She's the liberal in the family, a female chauvinist. She says she is going to have a career first and then maybe she'll consider marriage.

I told her that was fine by me. It's her life and I want her to do whatever will make her happy. And she shouldn't feel guilty if her poor old dad doesn't have any new places to hunt or fish.

She makes friends easily and runs around with a lot of strange people in their twenties. They do a lot of peculiar things like going to plays and art museums. There's not a single one of them with roots in the country. In fact, they think the country is something you have to cross as fast as possible to get to the next city. They wouldn't know a bass pond from a hole in the ground.

I've had many heart-to-heart talks with our younger daughter about her future. I've explained that she should broaden her horizons. There's nothing especially wrong with her running around with artsy-craftsy people but it would help her perspective if she knew some land owners. For instance, there's the Bartow boy, whose family is big in pulp wood and timber lands.

"You mean Noodle-Brain?" she asks.

This is where we usually start screaming at each other. I tell her she's prejudiced and if she really cared about people she'd try to help Noodle-Brain and take him to the art museum.

I don't know what's the matter with this younger generation. No matter how you try to help them, they just don't pay attention.

My Friend Has Gone

My friend is gone. He will not be back.

Some day I will go in his direction, and I hope to meet him there.

I don't know where old hunters go when they die. If we cross trails again, Fred will have a duck gun in one hand and a trout rod in the other. He'll wear a smile, with that excited anticipation a bird dog gets when he sees you take your shotgun out of the closet.

I miss him. I don't know if I grieve for him or for myself. Perhaps it does not matter.

For some reason, Fred accepted me at our first meeting, a dove hunt. I was flattered because he was a much better outdoorsman than I. That was many years ago, before I understood acceptance. I learned a great deal about it from Fred, a man blessed with great common sense, a shrewd observer of human behavior.

I suppose things were always black and white to Fred. He accepted me exactly the way he found me—faults, peculiarities, problems and all. He never tried to change me. He knew instinctively what it took me years to learn. We can change ourselves but we cannot change others.

For those he accepted, Fred had fierce loyalty. I think part of this was born in him and part acquired from the culture of the Tennessee mountains he loved so well. You're either fer somebody or agin them, and there ain't nothing in between.

Fred was an original. After all these years, I still catch myself trying to analyze his character, a complicated puzzle which not even his wife and children could piece together. Around most people he was an extrovert, but there was always a secret cache where his innermost thoughts were hidden. He did not share these, but sometimes I got a quick glimpse.

A lot of people thought he was a hard man, which he could be if the situation called for it. But I know about the day he had to take old Crock, his ancient golden retriever, to the vet to be put away. Fred tried to postpone the trip, but the dog, crippled by too many cold plunges, moaned at night.

Fred phoned the vet and asked to be met at the front door. He could not bear to go inside on the last walk with old Crock. There were tears in Fred's eyes as he sat in his car for an hour, waiting until he knew his friend was gone. And long after that dreadful day, I have seen his eyes watery when old Crock's name came up.

Fred never broke any records going to church but he was deeply spiritual, a fact which he tried to camouflage. He was one person in the city but a different man when floating a river for ducks or climbing far up a mountain to a hidden trout stream. I remember sitting with him once on a high cliff overlooking the East Tennessee Valley as the sun shimmered toward dusk behind low clouds. The golds, yellows, and oranges were fighting to crowd each other off stage as we sat silently for an hour, until it was pitch dark.

Finally, Fred whispered, "By God, that says it all!" He didn't say another word until we got to his truck over an hour later.

You could count on Fred for a practical joke on a hunting trip, not a mean one that would hurt people but one everybody could laugh at, eventually even the victim.

Years ago, in the goose fields around Lake Mattamuskeet, Fred took two of my friends to the pits. I had two others a hundred yards away, a hot blind where we quickly got a limit of honkers. A low flight of four headed toward Fred's blind and he timed it just right, the three hunters standing up together and blasting away. All four geese dropped.

It was five years before I heard the end of the story. Ray, whom Fred had guided, was fairly new to goose hunting but he still did not understand how Fred killed all four geese when his shotgun held only three shells. When the four geese fell, Fred ran into the field, dancing up and down, and claimed the birds. He did it so forcefully and convincingly the other two did not protest. Of course, they took their share of geese home but for five years Ray had wondered how Fred had managed to bag four for three.

I laughed and explained to Ray that Fred was good enough to bag a triple, but that was all. He had simply bluffed the other two gunners, just for the sheer hell of it. Most people would have cleared the story on the spot or at least that night. Not Fred! He never did tell them that they accounted for at least one of the geese or possibly two. He didn't care how long a joke had to boil before the point came out.

Fred hated to talk on the telephone. When I called him about a trip, he didn't ask a thousand questions and shilly-shally around. He'd say, "Where do you want me to be and what time?" I'd tell him and we'd hang up. He'd be there, right on the dot, even if it was a thousand miles away.

For several reasons, I always felt comfortable with him. He loathed pretense so I was always myself. I knew that if I broke a leg in a grouse wilderness Fred would get me out. I knew that if our duck boat turned over on a stormy lake we'd get ashore. Fred was there!

I knew that if there was one Vienna sausage left in the can he would insist that I take it. The harder it rained, the more Fred would laugh. As the trail got steeper, he climbed faster. The tougher it got, the more he liked it.

At times, I thought he used hunting and fishing as a narcotic, an escape from whatever inner conflicts may have troubled his great heart. If he had been born a hundred years earlier, he would have been a mountain man prowling the Rockies. Perhaps he is with the voyageurs or mountain men now.

It is strange how we can so enjoy a person for many years and never really know much about him. I do know I must accept the fact that he is gone. It is not easy.

Charged by a Dove

Mankind esteems him as the bird of peace, the symbol of benevolence, but to the hunter he's a feathered, frustrating devil.

The dove came jinking across the milo field on a westerly tailwind at a speed slightly over Mach 2. The sonic boom was drowned out by a barrage of No. 8s from hunters who popped up from their hiding places like Disney characters. As they scattered lead across the flats of Tulare County, California, the dove cut in its jet, flipped a wing, and double-clutched into a climb.

The ack-ack from more gunners was tracking the target, and I swung ahead and added three shells to the wastage as the dove disappeared—unharmed, unruffled, but not uncussed. It seemed to me that the bird was in league with the devil or in the pay of the ammunition companies.

Now, the dove is the universal symbol of peace, but this is truly ironic. No other bird approaches it in its ability to infuriate and frustrate mankind. In fact, it seems dedicated to exposing our inadequacies in the hunting field. Therefore, I have been overjoyed to learn that it has faults of its own.

The dove not only confuses and confounds men but makes liars out of them. One of my buddies is a college mathematics professor. When a dove shoot is over he can run a perfect tally of the birds he knocked down—but be absolutely incapable of adding up the misses. Strangely enough, he keeps track of my shooting and can tell me to a shell how far I went into the second box.

The dove brings out the sneaky side of human nature. I used to hunt with a city judge who was known far and wide for his probity and civic virtues, but he was not above pulling a fast one at a dove shoot. Before going to the field he slipped extra shells into his hunting coat. Then, at the beginning of a hunt, he'd break open a new box of ammo in front of us, elaborately count out fifteen shells, and put them in his coat pocket.

He always hunted at the far corner of a field, and it was his boast that he could get ten doves with fifteen shells. Time and again he proved it. Now, I do not blame the judge for this moral astigmatism, for he was an honorable man. Obviously the doves had affected that part of his conscience concerned with shooting.

A favorite trick of the peaceful dove is to charge the hunter. The flight comes in flat-hatting with full throttle and zooms right at the gunner. I have frequently been charged by doves and am not embarrassed to admit that I have resorted to prayer, especially since the day I saw a clergyman nervously telling his beads after he had been low-leveled by a large squadron.

The dove does particular injury to my pride, since I improve little from season to season. Each opening day I know I will make a public spectacle of myself, so I try to hunt far away from everyone. But it makes no difference. Somehow I always end up near two or three people who know me and, I suspect, shudder at my waste of shells. In fairness to myself, however, I must admit that I am a holy terror with the third box of ammunition. By that time there is no hope for a respectable score, so I relax in a what-the-hell attitude that gets results. If I could shoot the third box of shells first, I'd be one of the outstanding dove hunters of California.

The mourning dove does not play the game fairly. If you are jump-shooting from a field, he does not flush and fly in a predictable path at a constant rate of acceleration. It is his nature and inclination to be deceptive.

He leaves the ground much like a jacksnipe, acts as if he's going to climb, then puts on a burst of speed and swings out in an erratic curve. His is no smooth flight path like that of the quail or the pheasant. But I suppose one might expect this from a bird that builds flimsy nests.

Further evidence of the dove's furtive character is its ability to grow feathers that slip off in a retriever's mouth, a thing no dog wants any part of. So when old Rover runs to a fallen dove, he takes one sniff and comes back with an empty mouth. The owner sends him out again and begins to tell his shooting partners great stories of how magnificently Rover performs on ducks and pheasants. When this paragon refuses to pick up the dove on the second command, the owner explains that Rover *used* to fetch doves but has developed a mental block, or that it's too hot for dog work, or that doves don't smell like game birds, or that a good retriever does not like to change game, and so on. Meanwhile old Rover sprawls under a shade tree.

There is another way in which the dove erodes man's character— by impelling him to invent mendacious excuses when he returns to the car with a light bag, or none at all. He casually remarks that he does not care about dove meat; that the important thing is the sociability of the hunt, and not just the shooting; that getting away from the city and out into the country is more important than any limit. Each hunter listens respectfully and acts as if he believes every word. After all, any of them may run into poor luck next time out and need some of those excuses.

The bird of peace makes cowards of us all. I know one man who feels so insecure when he goes on a shoot that he always borrows a gun, thus providing himself with the ready-made excuse that he is shooting an unfamiliar gun which in no way fits him. Yet this hunter not only has a cabinet full of shotguns that fit him well but he is ordinarily an aggressive salesman of great diligence and fortitude. The dove has demoralized him. It would be uncharitable to find fault with this hunter; one must blame the bullying bird.

The dove even exacts its revenge when it hits the ground, dead. Lacking a good dog and working in heavy ground cover, it is easy to lose *any* dead bird; the dove hunter knows this and many even use the fact to advantage. When he straggles back to the car at the end of the day, with two doves in his vest, he laments the recovery conditions. Having knocked down eight doves, he says, he was unable to locate six, although he spent hours searching. Thus the truth is lacerated by a man who likely tithes each Sunday, is patriotic, and pays honest income taxes, but has been led by the diabolical dove into the tangled web of deceit.

Moreover, the bird of peace has been responsible for many broken friendships. Suppose two hunters—lifelong friends and neighbors—are standing side by side near a dead walnut tree awaiting incoming doves. A single comes zooming in, they shoot simultaneously, and the bird crumples. In the first glow of success each magnanimously tells the other to take the bird.

But suppose this happens three or four times. Or suppose one gunner bags nine birds, the other only one. What happens to their beautiful friendship? They don't speak on the way home; the next day their wives are snubbing each other; and within the week their kids are not allowed to play together. All because of the treacherous dove.

The dove, whose cunning knows no limits, fully realizes that there is safety in numbers. As I've pointed out, when a flight comes charging down an open stretch it is likely to demoralize the strongest character. A man must reach a decision right now—decide which dove to concentrate on, stick with it, and keep firing, no matter how many other doves appear larger, closer, or lower. He cannot waver, for if he hesitates all is lost. It takes great inner strength to make the decision and stay with it when the doves fan out in a flurry.

A hunting companion of mine from Atlanta is a successful business executive who keeps two telephones and a pair of secretaries busy as he solves problems and makes decisions that affect scores of people and huge sums of money. But what happens when this executive is charged by a flight of doves? Right—he hits the panic button. He swings from one target to another without pulling the trigger. He balks. He hesitates. He cannot decide which dove to take. Finally, when the birds are all around him, he swings the gun in a panoramic arc and gets off three fast shots at nothing in particular. Heaven help him if doves ever invade his executive suite!

The dove generates no end of evil. Suppose a broker has an unusually good millet field staked out. He invites a dozen of his most important clients for a shoot. There is plenty of feed, and the doves are concentrated by the hundreds. But that night a cold wave moves in and the doves move out. You can bet that the important clients will show up. And wait.

At three in the afternoon, no one has fired a shot. At four, a client walks over to his broker-host and asks grimly where the alleged doves are. At five, the hunters stomp out of the field—cold, bitter, and expressing doubt that the broker would be able to pick a winner in a one-horse race, let alone select a profitable portfolio of stocks.

All in all, the dove can drive hunters (a) nuts; (b) to drink; and (c) into bankruptcy. That's why all gunners love him. If you get a limit, you're obviously head and shoulders above the rest of mankind. And from there the view is fine.

It Takes Two to Plan a Hunt

Poor planning is often the reason for unsuccessful hunting trips. Sometimes a lack of planning can ruin an entire season.

A young couple I know is expecting their first child the last week of November. That's what I call poor planning. The last week of November is when the state's deer season opens!

The husband can't go out scouting for bucks ahead of opening because his wife might drop early. She'd never forgive him if he was out looking for tracks and rubs while she was laboring on another project.

Tom, the expectant father, can't plan to hunt for two or three weeks after the estimated time of arrival. His wife is an ever-loving doll, but she's never been on time for anything.

At their marriage ceremony two years ago, she came running down the aisle fifteen minutes late. She was holding up her skirt and yelling, "I do. I really do!"

Friends of the couple have a pool going on when the spoiler will arrive. I picked December 15. That was the latest date available.

If I'm right about a late hatch, Tom might as well give up on the whole season. By the time he gets home from the hospital and things quiet down, the deer season will be gone, rut and all.

Tom is facing a major loss, and he might as well grit his teeth and accept it. When your basic planning is wrong, you have to pay the penalty.

If the kid arrives on schedule, Tom will be sabotaged every year at the opening of deer season. It will be the kid's birthday. If the old man is not around for the candle blowing, it will cause disharmony in the home—like volcanic eruptions.

My advice to Tom is that it had better be a boy. When the kid is old enough to start hunting, about the age of three, the father can take him to deer camp every year as a birthday gift.

Young couples ain't as tough as they used to be. I remember years ago when Ellie Mae Hawkins showed up at a deer stand looking like she'd swallowed a watermelon. I don't know where her husband was, probably off bird hunting some place.

Ellie Mae suddenly went into labor, and when I went over to help she said we'd never make it to the doctor in time. A few contractions later, an eight-pointer ran right at us, and I nailed him. Ellie Mae screamed. It wasn't from the labor pains but because I stole her shot.

Things got awful busy, and I learned it wasn't hard to deliver a baby. I hoped Ellie Mae would name him Charles, but that was the last thing she had in mind. She still doesn't speak to me for shooting that buck off her deer stand.

Tom's been coming around and crying on my shoulder. He wants me to scout for him and locate some good runways or maybe a scrape. Then he'll duck out for a half-day hunt.

I turned him down flat. I've been caught in those scissors before. Some of the gray hairs on my head are from experience, not age. I like Tom and don't want to lose him as a friend.

Several years ago, when another wife was near birthing, her husband and I were in an extended discussion on the best hunting tactics for whitetail deer. The more health bars we visited, the grander the tactics became.

With each new milkshake, we picked up additional advice from other health addicts. By the time we got around to having bacon and eggs, I had several bets that I could kill a buck with a spear. My buddy was laying odds of five to three that he could run a deer down.

When we finally reached his home, all the neighborhood wives were coveyed up in his living room. After they gut-shot us with angry stares, one of them volunteered that my friend's wife had jumped the gun, and if he was interested he could go to the hospital and see his seven-pound son.

The father dashed off, but I made the mistake of not going with him. That was poor planning on my part. When he got to his wife's bedside, the first thing he told her was, "Charley kept me out all night!"

I haven't seen that kid to this day. The mama bought an attack dog and trained him on my picture, and I never go within a block of the house.

In the current case of poor planning, I've had a long talk with Tom, and he now understands that future editions should be published in July or August. That's well before the hunting season and allows some leeway. Besides, those are slow bass months.

I've also tried to discourage Tom from thinking he can sneak out hunting for an afternoon. Expectant mothers are not dependable. Thirty minutes after he left, his wife would be yelling, "My time has come!"

I've done my best to give him some fatherly advice. He's only been married to Pat for two years and doesn't realize that women have the longest memories of any species on earth.

"Look," I explained, "if that kid shows up while you're gone, you'll never be able to have a decent argument with your wife the rest of your life. No matter what the argument starts about, it will always end up that you weren't around when she needed you.

"She'll hit you with it five years from now, and on your silver anniversary, on your golden anniversary, and on your deathbed. Fifteen years from now, if you complain about the grocery bill it will wind up in an argument about your deer hunting when your first-born arrived."

Tom thought about that awhile. Then he said, "Well, I could always come back at her that she was late for her own wedding."

He's sure got a lot to learn about marriage.

Banking Memories

Fred always talks me into taking hunting and fishing trips I don't have time for.

If you can get him off the trout streams or away from his duck hunting, he's a brilliant criminal lawyer. When he wants my company for a trip, he's at his eloquent best.

He starts by telling me I'm such a jolly good fellow that he couldn't possibly have any fun unless I go. He anticipates my arguments that I can't afford the trip by preparing a brief of statistics showing how cheaply we can make it. Fred's a wizard at juggling *my* dollars! He quickly proves that it's cheaper to go with him than to stay at home.

Our relationship is a little peculiar. You see, we've never lived closer than five hundred miles. His home is in East Tennessee and I'm with a national company which is always moving me someplace else. I first met him in a dove field about fifteen years ago and since then have lived in a circle around him—in a number of different cities. While he has never come right out and said it, I think he decided to take me on as his pet charity case.

[205]

For over the years, Fred has talked me into meeting him in Idaho for chukar partridge, Quebec for grouse, Mattamuskeet for geese, and Louisiana for ducks. I didn't have the money or time to take any of those trips but Fred talked me into going.

I was always glad that I went although many of our trips were not to glamour spots and we've had plenty of rough, slow days. The point is that we went.

Being a trial lawyer, Fred has a bag full of tricks. He has used most of them on me, talking me into going despite a hundred reasons why I shouldn't. But now that I'm hooked, he mostly uses just one approach. It has been refined and polished over the years but it's basically what he told me on our drive to Valdosta.

After we were about an hour down the road, and had finished asking about families and mutual friends, he said, "I'm starting a bank account for you."

"You what?"

"Your problem is that you don't have a philosophy of life and ..."

"Who's got time for one of those?"

"That's what I mean," he said. "You're so busy picking up paper and moving it to another stack of papers that after a while you think it's really important. Have you ever run out of paper? When your stack gets low, doesn't another batch come in? After you're gone, won't the stacks of paper still be there?"

"Yeah, but you don't understand that..."

"I understand all right. That's why I want to explain my Memory Bank plan."

It goes like this.

When you open a Memory Bank account, you start making deposits. Every hunting or fishing trip you go on is a deposit. The more trips you take, even for a half-day, the richer you become.

You can withdraw any of the memories at any time, mull them over, relive them, and dream about them. There is no penalty for withdrawal because the memories go right back into the bank. There is no way you can lose on a Memory Bank account. It's a guaranteed account for life. Each memory deposit makes you a little richer.

The Memory Bank account is also for old age. When you're too old to get out of that rocking chair on the front porch, you rock gently and let the memories sift through your mind as a miser fondles gold coins trickling through his fingers. When you don't have enough strength to kick the cat out of the way, you can sink back and be glad you were farsighted enough to make a bonanza of deposits. It's an open account, always ready to draw on.

Of course, there's a catch. No one can make the deposits for you. No rich uncle can leave them to you. No one else can transfer his memory account to you. You have to make all of the deposits yourself. There will always be urgent, negative things trying to keep you from making deposits. Many obstacles will spring up to block you, but if you make the effort, you can become as rich as you want to. It's really up to you.

As Fred explains it to me, a man taking his short voyage on earth must develop a sense of values. What is truly worthwhile to him? When you yourself come to the end and look back, what will you say had true meaning? Will you remember that week of duck hunting at Currituck Sound or the mound of paper you shuffled the week before? Will you recall that magnificent buck standing on a crest in the purple sunset of New Mexico or will you remember the weekend you took a full briefcase home?

Now, please understand that Fred realizes a man has to make a living. He should! He's had his hunting and fishing interrupted often enough by having to go back to work and pay a few bills.

But when you get near the end of the line, what crossties will you remember? Do you think you will ever see an office as beautifully decorated as an oasis spring in the dry stretches of California where the quail and jackrabbits and coyotes come to ease their thirst? Though you visit all of the art galleries of Europe, where will you find one painting which will shake the marrow of your soul like a sunset bouncing off the sandstone cliffs of Utah? Will you ever find an expressway as lovely as a delta river fanning its way into the sea? Is there a city park as enchanting as a hidden lake in Alabama with wood ducks whistling their way through a canopy of cypress and tupelo trees? Is the exhaustion of watching two straight football games on TV as satisfying as panting your way through the snow trying to catch up with your beagles and a rabbit?

And, yes, what of the people? Will you remember those from the business cocktail parties or the guide in the Bitterroots who showed you your first bull elk? Will you harken up memories of people from your transient suburb or think back fondly on the guy you opened the dove season with every year? Who will remain in your Memory Bank account—the man who showed you how to write a good report or the buddy you got snowed in with for a week in Maine? Who are your *real* friends now? Are they the ones you joined on some business deal or the ones you sat with in the soft hush before dawn as decoys bobbled with scurrying whispers of rain?

When you are sitting on that front porch, a wool shawl over your shoulders, what will you remember? Will you think about the time the company gave you a big raise or remember getting a double on woodcock in Wisconsin as one of your best friends watched? And how your little setter merrily retrieved them? Is the watch they gave you at your retirement party as valuable as the memory of a sky full of pheasants flushing from the end of a cornfield in Nebraska? Or the time you were hunting marsh hens and fell into a hole of black mud? Boy, did your buddies ever laugh as you floundered out of the sticky ooze! Sitting there rocking and running out of time, will you wish you had put more in your Memory Bank?